REALIZING YOU'RE WORTH IT!

Advice, Insights, and Inspirations to Propel Your Career

Ha-Keem Abdel-Khaliq

First Edition
Published by Dream Publishing LLC
1. Non-fiction 2. Career Development
3. Employment Resources 4. Self-Help/Self-Improvement

Library of Congress Cataloging-in Publication Data has been applied for.

ISBN (Print): 978-1-66787-695-5
ISBN (eBook): 978-1-66787-696-2

CONTENTS

A Special Thanks...1

You're Worth It!..3

How to Use This Book..8

Advice

Take Time This Week to Develop Yourself 12

Write Down Your Year-to-Date Accomplishments 14

Share Your Career Story with a Leader 16

On the Road to Success, Don't Forget to Celebrate ...18

Take an Employee to Lunch 20

Get Meaningful Development Feedback
from Your Supervisor 22

Make Time to Unwind 24

Take Your Vacation 26

If You Want a Mentor, Be Specific as to Why 28

If Your First Thought Is to Write a Long E-Mail 31

Assume Positive Intent 34

If It's Out of Your Control, Stop Apologizing 36

Crazy Week Ahead? Breathe! 38

Ask for Help! 41

Have a Group of Advisors Who
Tell It to You Straight..44

Don't Recreate the Wheel 47

There Are Several Truths.
Don't Be Mesmerized by One.................49

Ask for What You Want.................................51

Take the Extra Thirty Seconds to Be Kind.................53

Lift Someone Up 55

Be Unapologetically Balanced 57

Be Unapologetically Driven 60

In All Ways—Other Than Your Values
and Manners—Be Flexible.................................62

If Every Career Choice You've Made
Has Been Wrong 64

Insights

Sometimes the Leader Isn't in Front.................................66

What Were Your Development
Expenses Last Year? 68

Are You Trying to Solve a
Complex Problem Alone?.................................70

The Best Person to Make *You-Time*? You. 72

The Best Way to Determine Your Career Worth 75

Career Advice I Would Give My Younger Self 78

Words DO Matter 81

It's Easier to Blame.................................83

You Don't *Have to* Have Fun at Work—
But It's Funner If You Do! 85

If I Had an Hour 87

If You Had a Chance to Do It All Over Again 89

Leaders Can Light Fires or Put Them Out 92

The More Questions I Ask, The More I'm Prepared ...94

You Don't Need to Burn Bridges to Win.
Build Them Instead. 96

You're Generally Only as
Good as Your Last Success...................................99

Enjoy the Stops................................... 102

Win or Learn................................... 105

Timing Is Everything, So Build a Good Watch 107

Being Polite Is a Great Career Move 109

EVERYONE Is Important in a
Successful Business 112

The Best-Laid Plans Often Fail. Adapt...................... 114

Meaningful Development Usually Involves Risk 116

How Many of Your Career
Barriers Are Fear-Based?................................... 118

There Is No Perfect Company................................... 120

Take Advantage of Opportunities 122

If You Don't Like the Ending, Write Your Own 125

What If Most People Want You to Win?...................... 127

Work Hard. Be Humble. Take Credit..............................130

If You Have to Ask, "Why Am I Here?" 133

Not All Stars Want to Manage.....................................135

Smile. You'd Be Surprised What Happens Next........138

It's Okay to Ask for Help 140

I Guarantee You: Someone Deserves It Less..............142

Your Time Is Valuable Too! 144

People *Are* Looking to You for Answers 146

Inspirations

Admire Problems. Create Solutions.............................149

It's Okay to Be Afraid of Success,
But Don't Let It Stop You!..151

Inspire 153

You Were Helped. Thank Them....................................155

You Were Helped. Help Someone.................................157

Go Ahead, End ALL Your Meetings
Five Minutes Early This Week! 159

If You Knew a Career Move
Would Be 100 Percent Successful 161

You Are Awesome. Now Prove It! 164

What Do You Wish People
Would Say About You? Do That....................................166

Be Original. Be Positive!..168

You May See a Future No One Else Does 170

Bet On Yourself–You're Worth It!................................. 172

The Next Chapter... 174

About the Author 177

A SPECIAL THANKS

Above all else, I give a special thanks to my wife, Erica, and my kids, Nakia and Tavian. They keep me grounded. I'll test ideas with them, and they give me honest feedback. If you've ever done something creative, you know how important it is to get feedback on your work of art, as well as how difficult it can be. They, along with my faith, are my rock when everything is unsteady. Thank you, family!

I want to thank my teachers. Throughout my schooling, I was blessed to have excellent teachers. Only now do I better understand the challenges they probably faced while they worked to inspire the best from my classmates and me. Thank you, teachers!

I also want to thank my bosses. Once anyone enters the workplace, it's possible to have a terrible manager. I've read about, seen, coached people through, and even helped leaders terminate some bad supervisors. Somehow, up to this point, I've yet to experience a bad boss myself. My experience has been the complete opposite from most people. My bosses have all taught me positive lessons that will stay with me for the length of my career. I've had direct and indirect bosses who have challenged me to be better, do more, and expect more of myself. It's with sincere gratitude that I extend appreciation and respect to my former and current managers.

Lastly, I want to thank the readers of my first book, *You're Worth It! Navigating Your Career in Corporate America.* We all have doubts. I'm no different. At the end of the publication process, I felt a lot of personal satisfaction for having completed my mission to write a book. But I wondered if the book would make a difference in the lives of others. I believe we're all here to help one another, and that book was a way I wanted to give back. I wanted to assist people in understanding how companies work and help them find their way in their careers. Then I read the reviews people posted online and realized how much they touched me. I received calls from people telling me how the book positively impacted their jobs. As I said, we all have doubts; seeing and hearing from readers confirmed that I was on the right path. You inspired me to write this follow-up book.

Thank you!

YOU'RE WORTH IT!

Who knew when we started this journey almost four years ago that I'd find myself with more to say regarding your career development? Yet here we are! Since writing, *You're Worth It! Navigating Your Career in Corporate America*, the response has been overwhelming. So many of you have let me know how the book has helped you gain that promotion, better understand business priorities, or even just what it means to actively manage your career. In addition, I've been invited to speak about career development at some of the largest companies in the world, to veterans' groups, to Boy Scouts groups, at dinners, at corporate events, at universities, and more. I had no idea there was such demand for an honest and straightforward summary of how organizations function and how anyone can use it to their advantage. So, why am I back to share more essential information that will help you with the next stages of your career? Let me explain.

Over these past few years, I've had several revelations. The first was that many employees weren't seeing their relationships with their companies for what they were. These employees believed they were in a personal relationship when they were in a contractual exchange. You are paid for the services you provide. Organizations often provide you with much more—including health benefits, retirement planning, career development classes, tuition reimbursement, etc. However, if you boil it down to its core, organizations pay you to work. No one builds up corporate capital for the number of years they've been with a company. What I mean by that is that it's not a reciprocal relationship. In personal relationships, both sides are expected to invest emotionally for the relationship to succeed. Many employees I coach mistakenly believe it's the same at their place of work. They think if they invest blood, sweat, and tears into the organization, they will be rewarded when it comes to layoffs or acquisitions. People think their efforts will ensure that they'll retain their jobs and continue their career arc in a similar fashion. Reality can hit people hard when they see the relationship for what it truly is— work. When I understood this truth, I was inspired to write the **Corporate Truths** that feature in my first book.

The second revelation I had resulted from my many conversations with employees, friends, family members, students, and other leaders when we'd come together to discuss career development. In those conversations, we discussed the importance of treating your career like an extended car ride. It seemed like a lot of people were taking everyday drives, but many did not know where they were headed or even if they were on the right road. In addition, many individuals felt like they were passengers in their own vehicles instead of drivers! They relied on supervisors, mentors, senior leaders, and others to provide them with career direction and development. When people have been working for years but suddenly conclude that they are no closer to their career goals, it's a shock that's similar to jumping into a freezing swimming pool—not an experience you want to have often. And yet, many people were plotting the same path forward without knowing their final destination. During our career discussions, I often found that a few minutes into our conversations, many people would begin writing down my suggestions or comments. Over time, I understood that I was shedding light on what felt like obscure topics. The more I reflected on those light-bulb moments, the more I was inspired to share my insights with as many people as possible, which became the source material for the **Worth It! Insights** in my first book.

The **Corporate Truths** and **Worth It! Insights** became the foundation for my first book. Once they were written and organized, it felt like I'd come to the end of my story as a career development coach and author. The truth was that I'd just gotten started.

I didn't see the third revelation coming. In many ways, it was right there in front of me, yet I couldn't bring it into focus. We often miss what's right in front of us. It was so natural to me that I didn't think twice about it. I've always known that I was a coach. For years, I've coached youth sports and corporate professionals. If there's an area that's always been a source of pride, it's that active listening comes naturally to me. I enjoy listening to people discuss their careers and guiding them on their journeys. Recently, during one such conversation, a thought crossed my mind that I'd not entirely given much credit to. As a coach, listening and providing insights are my greatest skills. These exchanges help me see the potential in people that they often do not see in themselves. Moreover, I help people believe in their potential. In many ways, through these conversations, I become a career cheerleader!

There are key career insights and lessons learned that have taken me a lifetime to understand. I've experienced them myself and I've seen people I've coached contend with them as well.

Over the years, they've emerged as key phrases that have been helpful to me and others. After the success of my first book, as more people asked me for advice, I decided it was time to put them to paper and continue the story. I just didn't have a plan for the story!

So, one evening in December of 2021, I sat in front of the computer and began typing. By the time I was done, I realized I was just shy of ninety pieces of advice, insight, and inspiration! Then, almost as suddenly as the inspiration came to me, it left. I was left sitting in front of my computer with words that felt special and meaningful, wondering what to do with them.

As the early winter weeks went by, I put what I'd written aside and relished in my favorite season. I listened to the Christmas songs that I listen to every year, and before I knew it, it was New Year's Day. Now, let me tell you, I'm not the kind of person who creates a New Year's Resolution every year. Instead, I'm typically the person who gets an idea and then tries to do it—regardless of the time of year. I've never needed an "annual fresh start" to get going. New projects and goals can always be established. I set little goals for myself almost daily. But as 2021 turned into 2022, I started brainstorming ways to connect with more professionals about career development. That's when it hit me: *Share what you've written with your LinkedIn connections*!

LinkedIn is one of my favorite professional tools. After I had written the manuscript for my first book, I reached out to my connections on LinkedIn and, through a series of exchanges, was empowered to self-publish my book despite having no prior experience doing so. LinkedIn is great for networking and professional growth. In my pursuit of coaching others, I decided to share my collected phrases on a regular basis. I had written enough for about nine months of inspiration. In the fourth month of sharing these insights and affirmations, I had yet another "a-ha!" moment. My pieces of advice, insight, and inspiration were the outline for my second book. It had been right there in front of me the entire time, and yet it took nearly half a year for me to see it!

While I wrote my first book from a teacher's perspective, trying to provide valuable lessons to people on their career journey, this book emerged with a different mission. Once we've warmed up and have started the game, we often need motivation, guidance, and insight to keep us going. As your career cheerleader, Coach Ha-Keem wrote the following pages to remind you that somewhere out there, you have a fan in the bleachers who's cheering you on.

HOW TO USE THIS BOOK

The following pages summarize lessons I've gathered throughout my years in business. In some cases, they represent many years of personal insight. Others are eureka moments I've captured and shared. Truthfully, many of the thoughts are not only suitable for your professional career journey but also your life's travels. I've organized the material in this book into three sections:

The *Advice* represents information that was shared with me at some point in my career—or information that *I wish* had been shared with me! It is also me passing along information that I've observed as useful throughout my career.

The **Insights** have come from conversations with other professionals and moments of inner reflection. Some are extensions of concepts in my first book. Like the insights from my first book, they are meant to help you from the inside out.

The **Inspirations** are challenges to propel you as a leader, meant to encourage and push you beyond what you currently see possible. Good coaches might motivate and guide you, but great coaches also provide encouragement. During my time as a career coach, I've realized that most often people stand in the way of their own career success. Sometimes people just need to see how spectacular they are to move ahead.

During the early 2000s, in their book *Built to Last,* Jim Collins and Jerry Porras popularized the idea of "Big Hairy Audacious Goals," otherwise known as BHAGs. Setting BHAGs for a company was all the rage. I ask you to do the same for yourself. After reading this book, set goals for yourself that you previously thought were unachievable.

As we prepare to dive in together, let me share a couple additional points. First, this book is meant to be read in no particular order. While I've organized this book into sections, each section has several short readings. Each was written to stand on its own, though recognizable themes are sprinkled throughout. It's *possible* to read this book in less than an hour; however, it's *impossible* to practice all the concepts in one sitting. Some of these will take time to weave into your career toolkit. When you first read a section, you may feel like it's meant *for you*. Once you put the ideas into practice, if you give the material a second reading, you might see it as being appropriate insight for someone you know. That is, if you come back to the material later, after it's helped you on your way, you might find its meaning has taken on a new tenor. Perhaps as you put things into practice, you'll find that some readings could help someone around you. If that's the case, please feel free to share this book with others. There's no right or wrong way to read this book. So read it cover to cover or skip around to what's most relevant to you at the moment.

Second, what's most important is the call to action. Each section and reading, in its way, is asking something of you. In that respect, I'm giving you a homework assignment. Hopefully, you didn't just set the book down and walk away. I know most of us don't like homework, but I've found that some of the best ways to practice a concept and understand it is at home alone when no one is watching. So, I ask you to first put the ideas to work in your mind. Write down answers to any questions or challenges you're being given.

That's it! You have everything you need to get started.

Ready?

Set.

Go!

ADVICE

TAKE TIME THIS WEEK TO DEVELOP YOURSELF

How many times have you uttered phrases related to your development that sound like:

"I'll do it when I have time?"

"If only there were eight days in a week."

"I'll focus on it as soon as I finish this project."

If you're like many of us, the answer is *too many times*. There is the classic story of the Cobbler. The paraphrased version of it is that there was a cobbler—a shoemaker—who worked in town. This cobbler made shoes for everyone in his village. Then one day, as he walked into town, he realized that everyone was wearing his shoes but his own kids. He had focused so much on others during his career that he'd forgotten about his family. At some point in our careers, most of us become the cobbler—if even just for a moment. We grow so focused on others, that we forget to focus on ourselves. We say it's just "for now," and that "it will be different eventually." But we fail to recognize that our tomorrow starts today. So, we must stop putting things off today. Today is about your tomorrow!

That's what this is really about—YOU! There's no time like the present to invest in yourself. The simplicity of saying *I am focusing on my development* is an important step. Start by blocking time on your calendar at a time that you are most likely to keep. Even start in small increments. Maybe you can't find sixty minutes. That's fine. So, look for thirty. If you can't find thirty minutes, find fifteen. You get the idea.

Don't delay. Start today!

WRITE DOWN YOUR YEAR-TO-DATE ACCOMPLISHMENTS

If you've worked in any job long enough, you'll realize that your performance will eventually be evaluated. It's a normal part of the performance-management process in most organizations. Often, this is called a *performance review* and is held at the end of the year. Over the years, I've come to realize that if I wait until the end of the year to summarize my activities and goals, I inevitably forget something. Worse, I might forget *many* somethings.

Think about the last couple of years working through the COVID-19 pandemic. In January 2020, the year ahead was optimistic for many companies and businesses. We all had our list of things we wanted to get accomplished. We may have even started some of the activities. Then, in March 2020, the world as we knew it changed and, in many ways, shut down. For months we were taking preventive measures to keep ourselves, our families, and our coworkers safe. Think of all the fantastic insights and achievements during that time. When December 2020 rolled around, how good were you at documenting all of them? Hopefully, you did a great job. However, much like best practices for planning and following through with career development, I've found it's good to be intentional when recording your performance.

What would that list look like if, every six months, you reflected on your actions? What if you kept a journal of these activities every three months or even monthly? How much better prepared would you be for your year-end review? I've even found that people are much better at explaining their role to peers and leaders across organizations when they begin putting this exercise into practice. Furthermore, however well-intentioned your manager may be, it's often the case that accomplishments and deeds haven't been recorded or remembered.

If you haven't started summarizing your work this year, I encourage you to start today! The work you put in now will be worth it!

SHARE YOUR CAREER STORY WITH A LEADER

This one may take a few of you out of your comfort zone. And I get it! How many of us are on a first-name basis with the leaders in our companies? Many of us have a very short list. How many of us would simply walk up to a leader we know and give them our career highlights?

First, to share your story, you must have a story to tell. In my first book, *You're Worth It! Navigating Your Career in Corporate America*, I share some of my thoughts about large companies and their obligations to key stakeholders. One of the concepts I share is that many companies have a goal to make a profit for these stakeholders. After reading my book, many leaders from various industries approached me to share that their company is not *only* focused on profits but on employees as well. While I hope that is true, if the company isn't profitable, then they won't have employees on which to focus for long. It's with this idea of company profits that I provide you with a possible area of focus for your career story—you!

Think about your job.

Now, think about the company. How does your job contribute to the company's success? If you aren't sure, ask your supervisor or your supervisor's supervisor. Keep going until someone can tell you exactly how your position improves the organization's profits. Once you are clear on your contribution, practice telling that story. How did you arrive at the company? Did you apply for a position? Did an agency reach out to you? What have you learned on the job? Where do you want to go in your career? What are some ideas you have that will improve the company's performance? And, at some point in the story, sprinkle in your year-to-date accomplishments and how they've helped the company achieve its financial goals. Add a few questions for leaders regarding their careers, the direction the organization is headed, and even about their families. Before you know it, you're ready to speak to any leader in the organization—whether that interaction is at lunch, at dinner, as people begin to log on to a video meeting, or even at the coffee machine.

Now, what *is* your career story?

ON THE ROAD TO SUCCESS, DON'T FORGET TO CELEBRATE

Type A. Workaholic. High flyer. Teacher's pet. Oh, ye who is so admired and reviled simultaneously—achiever be thy name! I've worked with so many people who fit this description. They always have a goal, and they are constantly seeking ways to beat those goals. They always seem to have the first six or seven years of their careers mapped out, and it seems they were born with a pretty good idea of who they want to be when they "grow up."

Whether you fit this profile or not, we all hope to experience consistent success throughout our careers. Our managers outline our goals for the year, and we spend the year finding ways to achieve them.

If we're fortunate, regardless of our personality type, we experience an abundance of success. Counterintuitively, when we experience success, we also need to learn to be cautious. So often, on the road to fortune, we forget the pit stops along the way—whether they are achievements or learning opportunities.

We make it to the mountaintop but forget the many mini wins along the way. I want to remind you to enjoy the journey.

There are several ways that you can get to Santa Barbara from Los Angeles. One of the more scenic routes is via Interstate 1. If your sole focus is to see how fast you can make the drive on Interstate 1, you'll miss the beautiful scenery along the way. That would be a shame.

It's the same with your career.

Rarely have I seen a person hit career goals without crossing critical milestones along the way. Those milestones are—and should be—moments of celebration. Consider them official points on the map of your career. They are reflection moments. They represent opportunities to celebrate an individual or a team. In addition, these are the perfect occasions to look back and realize how far you've come.

So go ahead, set outrageous goals. But pat yourself (and your team) on the back for the mini-pit stops. Celebrate them. And if you crush your objectives, crush the celebration!

TAKE AN EMPLOYEE TO LUNCH

Early in my career, I was fortunate to have met the CEO of several of the companies at which I'd worked. I didn't realize it at the time, but it was probably something they did often. However, it made me feel special. Whether I was special or not isn't the point. What mattered and made an impression was that a senior leader took time out of their day to get to know me—to know my name, my job, my background, etc. On several occasions, I was able to have lunch or coffee with these leaders. The meetings provided me with critical insight into the company's direction and "what kept them up at night." I could also share how I helped contribute to the bottom line. Ultimately, it may have cost them a few minutes, but it created a lifelong memory for me. If you're a senior leader, you can do this for someone in your company.

Close your eyes and reflect for a moment: How many pivotal people have helped you on your journey and gotten you to where you are today? How many moments were impacted by the leadership in your company? The career journey is long—filled with obstacles, unexpected turns, and a myriad of challenges. What if you helped remove an impediment for a current employee? Where would you start? Who would you choose?

A pastor at my church describes two types of people: "there you are" and "here I am." I'm going to apply this approach to leaders. "There you are" leaders can also be described as "servant leaders"; they take time to get to know people, regardless of their place or rank within an organization. Initially, it may seem like they are just playing the role of a good leader. However, it stands to reason that this approach provides a leader with quite a bit more than just great optics in relationships across an organization. It also serves as a feedback mechanism. Want to understand how a product is selling? Invite someone from sales to coffee. Want to know how the manufacturing line is operating? Invite someone from operations to lunch. These are opportunities to meet people and learn about a company qualitatively. It can also provide you with valuable knowledge about an organization's performance. At the same time, you're likely building a lasting impression on one of your future leaders.

So, who are you inviting?

GET MEANINGFUL DEVELOPMENT FEEDBACK FROM YOUR SUPERVISOR

Your supervisor is a valuable resource in your career. Outside of your peers, you undoubtedly spend most of your working time with your supervisor. In my last book, I shared the idea that not all supervisors like to provide feedback. In addition, even the ones who are okay giving feedback may not be great at delivering it. New managers all go through this in some fashion or another. Early on in a management track, it's not uncommon for people to wait to provide feedback, holding it until they are asked or for an End-of-Year review session. This approach to feedback often focuses on improvement areas and includes very little positive feedback. I'm overgeneralizing, but I've also heard from enough new managers to know there is quite a bit of truth here. Along the way, people realize that it's better to give feedback more frequently. If people share positive feedback more often than constructive feedback, it becomes easier to provide.

If you're lucky, you have one of those supervisors who frequently shares insights with you. The reality is, however, that many well-intended supervisors don't have time to give you feedback regularly. While that may be okay for some of you, it can become a distraction for others. Many employees have shared that getting performance or development coaching from their boss is like trying to extract teeth at a dentist's office—it can be pretty painful. But do not despair. Receiving feedback is a gift. You just may need to be creative to get it.

There are a few successful methods I've seen employees use in their pursuit for feedback. One of the easiest is simply asking your manager, "What would you have done in the same situation?" Their answer gives you a glimpse into how they think you handled it. Another way is having an open conversation about how you like receiving or providing feedback. If your manager tells you, "If you don't hear from me, it's a good thing," but you like to receive feedback frequently, you should engage in a discussion to determine who will adjust and how.

In the end, you are responsible for your development. But a good manager can provide you with valuable information that can assist you in reaching your goals.

What are you waiting for?

MAKE TIME TO UNWIND

There was a time when it was a *faux pas* to bring home to work. Home was home and work was work; you were expected to keep the two realities separate from one another. The past few years, especially in the shadow of COVID-19, have shifted the paradigm. I'm sure some of us have been on video calls where we've seen kids, parents, pets, or personal items in the background. Today, our personal lives are very much part of our professional lives and vice versa. It's in this space that I'd like to sit for a while—that space between home and work.

How many of us have had a bad day at work? How many of us have had a bad day at home? How often are those days the same day? Work can indeed be stressful at times. Have you heard the phrase "do more with less?" I'm positive it was first used within an organization or by someone who worked. We're asked to create more revenue with fewer resources. We're asked to build a better product with the same tools we've used in the past. And that's just at work. At home, we need to pay the bills, take care of family, get groceries, and the list goes on and on.

It's one of the reasons that I try to smile at everyone—at work or home—because you never know what stressors people have in their lives. And that's the point: It's really easy to have one or two things at work that cause stress. So, ensure you find the time to destress.

Unwinding is significant because it acknowledges that we have spent time "winding." Some people seem to have a never-ending reservoir of energy at work, but we rarely see that they take a 15-min walk over lunch to re-fuel. For some, it's working out every day; for others, it's a glass of wine and a good television series after work is done. Personally, I believe Europeans have it figured out. Over the summer, many friends I know in Europe take an annual vacation that's at least two-weeks long. And that's just their summer vacation. That sounds about right to me. What's right for you?

TAKE YOUR VACATION

The Oxford Dictionary's definition of vacation is: "An extended period of leisure and recreation, especially one spent away from home or in traveling." Operative words here: extended period. I spent most of the last advice chapter telling you to find time to unwind, and I mentioned vacation as one of the options. Paid time off is an essential part of the value offered by employers. I used to be an agency recruiter, and one of the benefits I would always encourage my candidates was to maximize their vacation. A good vacation hits a reset button in your mind and allows you to return to work fully energized.

It's important to call out that I'm asking you to *take* your vacation. I've seen many friends, colleagues, and family members continue working while on vacation. They go on their "holiday" with a cell phone, laptop, notepad, and a set of wireless earplugs so they can be fully "connected" to a place they've tried to "disconnect" from. I get it! Some of you are, in fact, CEOs, small-business owners, or top leaders in your organization. With so much responsibility, it's hard to be away. And to you, I still say, "You need a vacation too!" We all need time to recharge from work.

You're not a robot. Your body and mind need time to recover. You would be wise to listen to your body. Do any of you go on vacation and immediately become sick? I'm not a doctor, so I don't pretend to know how it all works, but I find it a strange coincidence that when you finally let go of some of the stress, your body forces you to slow down and recover. That may not be your ideal vacation, but it is necessary.

And let me add that I do believe in *staycations*. That is, stay at home rather than traveling while on vacation, but the rule of disconnecting still applies. Work on a home project. Write that book you've always wanted to write. Call your family and friends. Sleep in late. You get the idea. Take full advantage of not having to work so that when you return, you're ready.

IF YOU WANT A MENTOR, BE SPECIFIC AS TO WHY

We've all written the e-mail. A message to someone who may be a great mentor. It starts out something like, "Dear <insert name of person>, my supervisor has suggested that you would be a good person to potentially mentor me. I would like to schedule an hour on your calendar to discuss." Early in my career, I probably wrote at least five messages like this each year. Part of my development was getting to know individuals who might be able to help me in my career journey. It was great! I got the chance to meet leaders all over the company who would take an interest in my career. Invariably, I got the edge I needed to take the next two or three steps in my career. However, I rarely took the time to ponder why a person was a good match for me in my career. What expertise did they provide? How would the insights they provided assist me in my career aspirations?

I have been very fortunate throughout my career. I've met with countless senior leaders in the various organizations I've been employed, and all of them made time for me. I can't restate this enough—all of them! Imagine receiving an e-mail from a new employee asking for an hour of your time. If you're a senior leader, you know how much "free time" you have in your day. The answer is likely "none," yet these leaders found a way to spare sixty minutes to speak with me about my development. I'm sure I asked somewhat insightful questions, and I don't recall the time passing slowly. Yet, as I reflect on those times today, I realize that my time may have been better spent knowing why I wanted to speak with them and using the time to focus on that purpose. It would have been a better use of everyone's time. I come to that conclusion because, as much as they all influenced me, I'm no longer in touch with any of the senior leaders I met with during those early days of my career. Even if I wanted to reach out, I have few direct ways to be in touch with them.

The truth is that early in my career, I didn't know who I wanted to be. Some of you do, and that's great. But many people leave school without a clear understanding of who they want to be when they grow up. It would have been better to simply call those early mentoring calls what they really were: networking calls. They could have been done over a thirty-minute coffee session. Across many subsequent meetings, I realized that I wasn't the only one navigating murky and unclear "mentor" rules. Many of us have had the same mentor conversations without truly knowing what we were there to accomplish.

Mentor/mentee relationships are a commitment by both parties. Before engaging in them, take the time to assess your goals. If your manager suggests someone as a mentor, then question your manager as to what precisely this person has to offer. Question if and why they are a fit for you. If your manager cannot answer the question sufficiently, you may decide to meet with them anyway, but reframe the meeting for networking purposes.

Before taking the mentor plunge, do your homework. The time spent upfront will go a long way toward helping you achieve your career goals.

IF YOUR FIRST THOUGHT IS TO WRITE A LONG E-MAIL

Go with your second thought!

We live in a world dominated by social media and technology. Even if we sincerely wanted to leave technology behind entirely, there are few ways to do so. We're entrenched in thoughts, opinions, perspectives, pictures, instant gratifications, emojis, and the list goes on and on. Technology and the way it's fed our increasing "connectedness" is an important backdrop. Even before COVID-19, there was the sense that people were taking in and sharing more information than ever but growing increasingly disconnected every day. You see it in politics, on TV, in newspapers, and in online articles daily. Insert a flashy catchphrase title, add a few lines, use the words *Us* and *Them*, and wrap it up with a good ol' fashioned summary that has a few dashes of judgment, and I've probably described most of the content you've seen since the 2008 U.S. election. Twelve years of increasing vitriol and then 300M—pandemic! If we struggle to truly engage with each other outside of work, then how do we communicate *at work?* It will be a miracle if we can talk with one another again, which is why I think it's important to buck the trend at work. At work and across our careers, we must find ways to meaningfully communicate!

Your boss doesn't get you. A customer wrote a complaint against you. A coworker doesn't fully understand the situation. Whatever the reason, as you pound on the keyboard, banging out *the e-mail of all e-mails* that will put everyone in their place, pause for one second and ask yourself, "What am I doing?" If someone wrote a full-page e-mail to tear you down, should you really take two pages to respond? Do you find yourself thinking: "If I just capture all the relevant points in my e-mail, *then everyone else* will understand." If so, please stop writing and reconsider. Or send the message *to yourself exclusively* to let off steam and process whatever you're feeling.

These e-mails almost always include several recipients, copied in on the message just for impact. You might intend to let everyone know how ridiculous the other person's e-mail or action was. I get it! And I've been there. However, the fact is that no one usually looks good in these situations. The other eight or nine people copied are usually dumbfounded that they are a part of this e-mail train. Most people just wonder how things got so out of hand and why someone didn't just initiate a call to solve an issue before it became an awkward problem.

If you find yourself licking your lips before you type your e-mail response, consider alternatives. Drop into an office for a chat. Give them a call. Send them an Instant Message to see if they have time to talk. You will build a better relationship and likely get to the resolution much faster. In a world of automation, robots, technology, and digital distance, be the person who seeks personal connections. In a world of problems, instead of sending the long, passive-aggressive e-mail, be the person who says, "Houston, we have contact." Create contact!

ASSUME POSITIVE INTENT

Ever read an e-mail and think, "This person is yelling at me in this message?" Or have you tried calling someone, and realized that their phone immediately went to voicemail, so you know they intentionally had to swipe to decline the call? What is your first thought after that? Did you think, "I'll show them!"

Or do you approach things differently? Before you rush to judge, do you maybe wonder if it's a bad time or bad day to be in touch? You'd be surprised how often e-mail, facial expressions, and things *not said* impact how we feel about a person or situation. I've seen scenarios like these escalate so many times, but one particular event has stayed with me for years.

I was working on a global team, and one of the business leaders opposed the company's direction. This business leader had previously voiced many strong opinions, but this time felt different. It seemed like they were "digging in their heels" and preparing for a fight. In fact, they'd gone so far as to enlist support from others in the region. Battle lines were being drawn, and many of them were against the president of the business. Leaders across the business had given snippets of insight to the president, so people were prepared for all-out war. Once I'd heard comments from all sides of the organization, I approached the president and asked, "How do you intend to handle this one?"

The answer was something I'll never forget. "I'm going to assume positive intent and talk to them directly." In other words, "I'm not going to worry about gossip. I'm going to talk to the individual in person and form my own opinions. In addition, I'm going to assume they are coming from a good place concerning our business." That mindset changes everything.

We all have disagreements at work. But, what if as part of addressing those disagreements, you could assume the other person was coming from a good place? What if you just needed to better understand the other person's position? Come at things with the assumption of positive intent, and you'll be surprised how your work—and life—interactions change.

Is there someone you need to try this with today?

IF IT'S OUT OF YOUR CONTROL, STOP APOLOGIZING

"Sorry for joining late."

"Sorry, you didn't understand my e-mail."

"I apologize in advance for scheduling this meeting, which is critical to our customer."

Any of these sound familiar? Have you been in situations where you've apologized for things that are entirely out of your control? For example, you are scheduled in back-to-back meetings all day, and after one of those meetings, you take a break to go to the bathroom or grab a quick bite to eat, which causes you to be late in joining the subsequent call. Do you immediately apologize for joining a couple of minutes late? If so, you may want to pause and think about what you're apologizing for. If you scheduled your own day with back-to-back meetings, it might be an opportunity to rethink your scheduling practices, but certainly not something you need to apologize for. If someone else requested that you attend meetings and your calendar fills up, then it's reasonable that you take a break to eat or use the restroom. The point here is that while it may come across as polite, when you say that you're sorry for events that are beyond your control, you assume blame when it's not earned. That is, you end up assuming misplaced blame.

Have you ever invited a friend to a party, and by the end of the night, that friend is completely out of control and causing a ruckus among the other partygoers? On your way out, you grab your friend and apologize to the organizers and others who the person may have offended. Why do we do this? There are many reasons, I'm sure, but one of them is likely that we're embarrassed by their actions. *They* may not have apologized, so *we* feel obligated to do it on their behalf even though we did nothing wrong. Again, if this person has a history of doing this at other parties, it may be that your judgment could be called into question, and you may be culpable at some level. However, if this isn't typical, then the individual should apologize *not you*. Sure, it's polite, but in reality, you are tying someone else's behavior to your own. You are accepting blame for something outside of your control. In careers, I've seen this habit of accepting blame diminish the confidence of talented leaders and even create severe misperceptions.

Your time is valuable. You're human. The next time you feel the urge to apologize, assess the situation. Are you truly at fault? Was your behavior reasonable? Have you mis-stepped in some way? If not, just say, "Hello, everyone," and go from there!

CRAZY WEEK AHEAD? BREATHE!

It's Sunday evening, and you dread going to bed because you know what's ahead of you this week. Your week is filled with meetings. You have an important presentation that may make or break your team's ability to achieve its goals. You need to have a difficult conversation with a supervisor or direct report. There are any number of situations that can cause angst. That anxiousness can cause you stress. It can keep you awake at night, leading you to miss out on valuable sleep. We all know that a good night's sleep can help us perform better. Whereas, an awful night's sleep with little rest can cause us to be short with others. After a sleepless night, you might be more irritable than usual, so you might bark at someone with whom you'd normally have a collaborative conversation.

If you've been working long enough, most of us have experienced quite a few situations like these. It can be challenging to function. At such moments, perspective and self-awareness matter. Breathe and focus on putting one foot in front of the other until you make your way through the challenges.

Work puts all of us in situations that can cause stress. There are many conditions during a typical workday that put us in uncomfortable situations. I have some things that help me get through most of these settings *relatively* unscathed! The first is understanding my triggers. This concept was shared with me by a coach who helped our team understand interpersonal dynamics and find ways to improve them. We all have triggers—things that set us off, even if we're not aware of them. It could be there's a coworker who always asks you a disruptive question during meetings, even though you specifically engage with them ahead of time to understand what questions they might have. It could be the leader that never makes it through the pre-read and then spends most of a meeting asking questions that were carefully addressed in prepared documentation. The list goes on and on, but whatever your trigger, they can put you on edge and cause you to act differently than usual or even impulsively. Understanding your triggers can allow you to anticipate them. They can also help you become self-aware. Once we're aware of our triggers, we can proactively manage them or avoid them altogether.

The second technique I've found helpful is focusing on one thing at a time. There is the famous Chinese proverb, "The journey of a thousand miles begins with a single step." I have found that putting this proverb into practice has helped me to remain calm under intense pressure. Break things down into smaller pieces. You may have forty meetings this week, but what do you need to prepare for the first one or two? After that, what steps are required for meetings three through five? And so on. By breaking the challenge into smaller parts, they become more manageable.

Oh, and if things are spinning entirely out of control, don't forget to breathe. Have you ever noticed how instinctive it is to hold your breath when things get tough? It's incredible how often stress influences our breathing.

Take a deep breath. You got this!

ASK FOR HELP!

In elementary school, we had teachers who helped us learn to carefully navigate the world. They showed us how to play with others, sit quietly at our desk, line up, take turns, clean up, and even when to take a time-out—be it voluntary or not! As we transitioned from middle school to high school, and then up into university, there was a teacher or professor who guided us, told us what we needed to know, or pointed out where we might need more support. At the same time, there were counselors available that could help guide our learning journey.

Things shift when we leave school. When our formal schooling ends, there's no one whose job it is to tell us what must do to be successful. There's no longer someone "in our corner" to assist us on our learning journey. In many ways, when we leave school, it's as if *we've arrived!* We're just unsure of the destination at which we've arrived.

It usually takes us a while to realize that as we get older, we reach the stage in life where we're responsible for our own successes and failures. No one tells us how to win; we get to figure it out on our own. The problem is that there are multiple avenues we can take. We all encounter situations in our career where we'd benefit from the insights of a trusted guidance counselor. When faced with many options, risks, and considerations, what are you to do?

This is the exact time when you should ask for help. The answer may seem obvious, but it's something many of us resist doing. Have a deadline that requires a top-notch PowerPoint presentation? Who do you know with great PowerPoint skills who can help? Have to give a speech in front of new hires about navigating their careers? Talk to someone who has given quite a few speeches and ask for tips. Have twenty projects in which you are expected to lead the teams to completion, but you are unsure where to start? Check with your supervisor, a peer, a project manager, or a mentor on prioritization ideas.

Somewhere along the way, after our schooling was over, we accepted the notion that we must tackle all our work situations alone. Somehow or another, we assumed self-reliance made us tougher. Or perhaps we started to believe that we were better employees if we could find the solutions ourselves. This could not be further from the truth. We all need help at work and in our careers. None of us arrived at our current situation alone.

Sure, we may have made decisions that we wish we could take back; however, even those decisions were likely made with the best information we had available at the time. And those are the operative words, "The best information we had available at the time." To have the best information, we must check what we know—or don't know—with others. When we assume we have all the answers, what does that say about us? Is it slightly arrogant to assume we know everything? When we engage the minds of others around us, we gain the advantage of their collective wisdom. If the people around us think differently than we do, is there insight we can gain from their perspectives? It's likely that we can benefit from their unique experiences.

Let's look for a relatable analogy. If you're at the gym lifting heavy weights as part of a workout, you'll likely ask someone to spot you, right? At the gym, you seek out a spotter—someone to watch you and help guide or remove a weight if it becomes too heavy for you to lift. We need spotters at work too. In your career, if you find yourself carrying too much weight, find a spotter and ask for help.

If you're in that situation right now, who can you go to for advice? Who's your spotter?

HAVE A GROUP OF ADVISORS WHO TELL IT TO YOU STRAIGHT

If you take away nothing else from this book, I want you to know that _I believe you will be successful_. To find success in your career, you will need someone—or several someones—in your life to tell you when you're heading in the wrong direction.

There's a well-known phrase we should all take to heart: "The enemy of future success isn't failure but past success." When someone achieves success at early points in their career, it can be difficult to understand that if they keep doing the same things, successes are not guaranteed to continue. Past success does not guarantee future success. We need more than one toolkit during a long career. Embracing this reality is hard; when we experience success, we expect it to continue. We think that if a process or set of skills has helped us achieve success once, that it will always ensure smooth sailing. That's at least one reason we all need a _career trust group_ that includes someone who is a straight shooter. We need someone to tell us the truth when we can't see it.

Your career trust group is a person or set of people who are familiar with you on a professional level. They've known you long enough to tell you when you're off-center. The individuals in this group are your advisors. Some of them will give you advice that you always take. Some of them will give advice that you never take. They will provide a perspective on your current professional situation and the options you have in front of you. Members of your career trust group are unafraid to give their opinion. Now, I'm not talking about the friend who is unabashedly blunt about everything and may even be a jerk! And I'm not talking about the friends who never challenge your position or tell you that every decision you make is the right one. Your career trust group should help you find your equilibrium when your career is off-balance.

One of the most difficult things people have shared with me as they've advanced in their careers is that the higher they climb, the fewer people they have to consult about the challenges they face. As I wrote in my last book, leaders don't always have the answers. Everyone needs a coach, mentor, or career cheerleader to encourage them to keep pushing forward even when the path ahead is not clear. Everyone needs a career trust group to let them know when they are not being true to themselves. Building that trust takes time, so if you don't have a group on whom you can rely, start looking for people with whom to connect.

The good news is that this group can consist of nearly anyone. It can include a sibling, former boss, or professor—whomever. The important thing is that you begin bringing them into your career decisions early. Just like anything, it will take practice to find the right combination. You may have to try out a few candidates before the right trust group appears. Though it doesn't have to, it's also possible that the group may change or evolve over time.

Now that you know the criteria, who are the first five names that come to mind for your career trust group? Start with them.

DON'T RECREATE THE WHEEL

I'll let you in on a little secret about me: Before I try something new, I check it out with just about everyone. There have been countless others before me on career paths similar to mine. I love researching solutions to problems that others have already solved. Instead of reinventing the wheel, I'll reach out to peers. I'll read news articles. I'll have brainstorming sessions. If people I know have been in a similar situation, I'll listen to their ideas. It's not that I don't like being creative; I do. Rather, I have found that by bringing in the experience of others, I can learn what worked and what didn't. I can gain valuable insight and different perspectives on a problem or challenge. In the end, if the problem warrants it, I'll come up with a novel solution. But many times, I'm able to take an existing good idea, create a variation of the concept, and apply it uniquely to my situation. These steps help me avoid putting too much energy into something that's already been created. Why create a new path if one already exists?

For example, I was working on a project recently. We were trying to build an application that would allow us to assess the talent within the organization. We had defined the problem. We engaged the appropriate resources. We asked consultants and organizations that we trusted if they'd ever heard of or encountered an existing application that fit our requirements. The answer was no. We checked out the applications people claimed to use for similar needs. No one had an off-the-shelf solution that fit our precise requirements. From there, we spent the next six months building an application. When we were near completion, we happened to network with someone in another business and learned they had created a similar application. They'd finished their application not six months before. My heart sank into my gut. We spent countless hours building something that was already made.

In the end, the work was worth it. We ended up utilizing insights from both applications for our final outcome. Still, the process underscored the importance of communicating actively and effectively when seeking answers.

There are many times in your career when you will need to do something that's never been done. At those times, you'll need to walk a road that's never been walked. At those times, other people's experiences may not be helpful as they may not inform whatever scenario you are facing. However, those career moments are few and far between. It's much more likely you'll be asked to solve an issue someone else has previously solved. By asking around, you'll gain the collective experience and brain-power of the various leaders around you. This can save you vital time, energy, and potentially frustration.

Is there a wheel you are currently reinventing? Are there other ways to tackle the problem? If so, who do you know—or better yet, who don't you know yet—that can assist you in your efforts?

THERE ARE SEVERAL TRUTHS. DON'T BE MESMERIZED BY ONE.

Have you ever been part of an investigation at work? There is a complaint, and one employee claims this or that happened. You gather a few people and start interviewing the involved parties. When the interviews are complete, you realize there are multiple ways to view the evidence. As information emerges, and you see things from different points of view, it's possible to understand how each party believed they were right. In other words, there is more than one truth. If you perform enough of these investigations, you realize that there are often many versions of the truth. We do ourselves a disservice when we become beholden to only one version.

In one of my previous companies, I had an employee that asked me to be a mentor. I take these requests quite seriously, so before I accepted the invitation, I wanted to understand why they wanted a mentor. The employee shared with me where they wanted to go in their career and why I would be a good person to assist them. I ultimately accepted the invite and, over the next year, we'd meet whenever they wanted to connect. In time, I noticed a pattern. As they shared details of their work life, I realized that most accounts included how their direct supervisor was holding them back. In one of the discussions, I presented the idea that maybe what was holding them back was how they viewed the interactions. That is, the supervisor's approach was secondary, and what was primarily holding back my mentee was their own perspective. After an initial denial, my mentee listened to the explanation I provided. Without going into all the details, I shared a different point of view on the various scenarios. Eventually, the employee agreed that maybe they were getting in the way of their advancement. I've experienced numerous encounters such as this one, and the result is typically the same. When you show people how the same situation could be perceived differently, it expands their understanding. This also plays out in team dynamics and is why having a team full of diversity is so important. There are always multiple perspectives, experiences, and truths.

If I work on a team where everyone has the same background, we'll all have the same blind spots. But a team full of multiple experiences benefits the entire team. Another person's strengths can cover my weaknesses. Various points of view can be shared, and we can leverage the best ideas at critical times.

In your career, strive to create or be a part of teams that seek multiple points of view. Avoid or try to positively influence situations where people are almost blindly focused on one source of truth. If you're in a meeting and see a potential business plan pitfall, speak up and share your thoughts. Be a champion of different perspectives and truths.

ASK FOR WHAT YOU WANT

There used to be a commercial that started with a highlight reel of all the clutch shots that Michael Jordan made. The successes were followed by a montage of shots he took that did not go in. The commercial was probably to sell some drink or some shoe, but the real point was to tell you that he took the shot. He missed way more shots than he made, but he was unafraid to take the shot again and again. That's why he won. As the famous saying goes, "You miss 100 percent of the shots you don't take." I see a similar pattern in our careers. I've been in Human Resources for some time now, and I've spoken with hundreds of professionals who have shared how they are undervalued. Some of them are colleagues, some of them are just friends, and some are employees looking for guidance. Others are just about to enter the job market and want to ensure they start off on a good foot. Invariably, in one form or fashion, I end up sharing a core piece of advice with all of them: Remember to ask for what you want. In other words, take the shot.

This may seem like advice that's easier said than done, but I tend not to think of it that way. You would like a $10,000 raise. You believe that you've put in the work and time; many times over, you have demonstrated your ability to create value for the organization. What's keeping you from asking for the raise? Would it surprise you to learn that many people don't ask simply because they don't want to inconvenience their manager? For others, it's the fear of having the reply be a firm "No."

But let's look at it a different way. Another possible outcome is that they say "Yes." What if they say, "Not know, but soon?" There are likely as many potentially positive outcomes as there are negative ones. And by negative, I mean all the options where you don't get the raise. You may set the wheels in motion to get the raise by simply asking the question.

You miss 100 percent of the shots you don't take.

Take the shot!

TAKE THE EXTRA THIRTY SECONDS TO BE KIND

The last couple of years have been unlike any others that I can recall across my career or life. You have a global pandemic, people yelling at and judging one another due to their political affiliations, families disowning one another on social media, high unemployment and massive layoffs, low unemployment, vaxxers and anti-vaxxers mad at one another, natural disasters at seemingly epic levels, some people living almost solely in front of a computer screen—and this is *just the highlight reel* from the past few years, not a fully comprehensive list! That doesn't even begin to tell the story of personal relationships, lost family members that we couldn't spend time with for risk of getting infected or infecting others, the financial burdens we face, etc. In all of this, we're supposed to go into work as if we aren't carrying the weight of the world on our shoulders.

There used to be a time when you went into work and you left your personal stuff at home; then, when you went home, you left your work stuff at the office. If we're honest with ourselves, though, we know the boundaries between work and home were never very rigid. No one has ever been *entirely successful* in compartmentalizing personal stuff and work. We brought work home and home to work. It was inevitable. It was an illusion to say otherwise. If there is something that's been wonderful about COVID and the remote-work environment, it's that now you can't help but see people's home lives while they are at work. During video meetings, I've seen people's dogs walk over and start licking my colleagues. I've talked to coworkers' kids while at work. I've seen family photos in the background of calls. I've seen more than one person need to stop a call abruptly because of something happening in their home. I love it! We get glimpses into the lives of people with whom we work in a way that seemed hidden before. It helps us understand each other better. And all of this is important because we need to understand each other more than ever today.

Even if we see people on the screen, we have no idea what they are going through unless they tell us. It's been a tough few years for us all. What if we all committed to start each meeting by asking how everyone is doing or checking in on one another? Now more than ever, we all need to be checked in on. We need to show each other that extra little bit of empathy. We need to take some time to be kind.

I just really believe that.

LIFT SOMEONE UP

Today, it's easy to become enthralled by our own circumstances. We carry around these distracting little devices, which are really mini-computers, that give us access to nearly limitless and instantaneous information. Many people now have the ability to work from home. We can have groceries and prepared meals delivered to our homes. Clothing can be shipped from anywhere in the world to our doorsteps. During the height of COVID-19 lockdowns, many people realized that if anyone wanted to build a life with limited to no contact with others, technology had pretty much made it possible.

But therein lies our opportunity. What if you *were* on your own, and you needed help? We shouldn't be looking for ways to distance ourselves from each other. We should be doing the opposite. If you stumbled upon someone who was stuck or needed your assistance to move past whatever obstacle they were facing, what would you do? In this age of digital distance, how do you even know if someone in your circle needs help? Let's assume that *someone* needs your help. Are you able to help from home?

If you're reading this book, it is my sincere wish that you are on a path that will bring you great joy in your career and life. That said, wherever you are, there's a good chance you didn't get here by yourself. Someone lifted you; someone helped you get to where you are. It could be that your parents took extra jobs so that you could go to college. It could be that there was a teacher who took an interest in you and pushed you past what you saw as your limits. Whoever it was, someone—or many people—helped you take the steps to where you currently find yourself. It may not be where you ultimately want to be, but you're on a journey that has been supported by others. It's important to give back. Somewhere out there is another person who needs guidance and support to move forward.

Let me take this moment to say that great teachers are truly underpaid. I don't know what must happen to change this, but I would gladly give up watching any reality show where the participants are paid millions so those funds could be redirected toward the great teachers who positively impact the lives of our youth.

Show gratitude to the great teachers you know by showering them with actual thank yous, gifts, and financial support. Become a mentor, sponsor, or coach to someone. Let those around you know that you're willing and able to help.

BE UNAPOLOGETICALLY BALANCED

I've had colleagues who were not in their jobs for the money. Don't get me wrong, they made good money, but they weren't living to work, they were working to live. One of them used every opportunity to go on vacations worldwide. Another wanted to build up enough vacation to ensure they could take most of the summer off to visit family. Another needed to be home when their kids left for school and when they returned from school. Each of these colleagues was good at their job. If they wanted, each of them could have made sacrifices in their personal lives that could have quickly gotten them further in their career, but they were perfectly okay with their trajectory. What motivated them was balance in their personal lives and career.

There used to be a time, not that long ago, when supervisors would walk around looking at people's desks early in the morning and late in the evening to see if people were at work. These managers would use that information as a proxy to determine if members of their team were hard workers or not. To be honest, I'm aware of some managers who continue some version of that practice even today. But when COVID happened, priorities at work changed almost overnight.

I won't say that COVID caused The Great Resignation or led to organizations realizing that their employees could successfully work from home. I will say that the onset of a global pandemic forced individuals and organizations to think differently. It gave people time to reflect on their careers. It forced companies to look at alternative solutions to support productivity. Then people started quitting! Many companies experienced a mass exodus.

I read article after article explaining why people were leaving their jobs. Quite a few employees switched industries. Many wanted to find a better balance. If you decided to make a change during The Great Resignation, I congratulate you! However, if you haven't taken a step to find your career equilibrium during the past few turbulent years, I encourage you to connect with friends, mentors, family, or others in your network for ideas that will help you set new, balanced routines.

So many organizations now fully get this and are better prepared than ever to help team members set a balance between the personal and the professional. I've seen better maternity and paternity leaves. I've seen a multitude of hybrid-work arrangements. If you need a change in your career to establish more balance in your life, there are options. There may be options for flexibility with your current company, or you might find a new position that's a perfect fit. The right company and position are out there for you. Determine what you value and prioritize. With that set, you'll ensure that you can find the balance in your career and personal life!

#UBU

BE UNAPOLOGETICALLY DRIVEN

I happen to know and have worked with a lot of entrepreneurs in my lifetime. It's fair to say that some of these individuals spend more time at work than most. If they're not at work, they're thinking about work and how to make it work better. They eat, sleep, and dream about their businesses. It makes sense. An entrepreneur's business is their passion, not just a source of income. We all seem to understand that these self-employed leaders will spend an enormous amount of time at work. However, do we show the same understanding to the employee who is passionate about their career? Sometimes, we give those individuals sideways looks and warn them about burnout. In many cases, we're not wrong to warn them. But do we also support them and their passion?

This is a complex topic because I know it is possible and relatively easy to experience burnout in your career. The person who spends all their time at work—entrepreneur, corporate professional, or person staying home to take care of their kids—is susceptible to feeling fatigued about their job. These people need to find balance. If you are a colleague, manager, or friend, look out for people on the brink of burnout. Give them good advice about striking the right balance between job and rest. But what about the people with an unending reservoir of energy at work? When people are highly focused on succeeding in their careers, and seem to never tire, what advice do we give them?

About ten years ago, there was a leader of an investment banker firm who said something like, "You don't come to work for us to find work-life balance. You work for us to make a lot of money." Now I'm not here to tell anyone who went to work for him that they're doing the wrong thing. My guess is many people walk into situations like that with their eyes wide open. As they should, if that's their priority. And I would still caution the highly driven folks out there that something eventually gives—whether it's relationships, friendships, or physical and mental health. My advice to the go-getters is to keep a good group of friends and advisors around them to ensure they stay okay.

If you are one of those individuals who wants to climb the corporate ladder quickly, grow your business, or gain as much experience as possible in a short amount of time, and you're willing to put in a lot of extra time to achieve those goals, *then go for it!*

Be safe. Take care of yourself. Be aware of your impact on others. And be unapologetically driven.

#UBU

IN ALL WAYS—OTHER THAN YOUR VALUES AND MANNERS—BE FLEXIBLE

Your career journey is going to produce lemons. There's no getting around that. There's a line in *Rocky Balboa* where he is talking to his son about how to deal with life. He tells him,

> "*Let me tell you something you already know. The world ain't always sunshine and rainbows….and I don't care how tough you are, it will beat you to your knees and keep you there permanently if you let it. You, me, or nobody is going to hit as hard as life. But it ain't about how hard you hit—it's about how hard you can get hit and keep moving forward.*"

The rest of the speech is just as inspirational. He talks about going out and getting what you're worth, but to be prepared for the hits along the way.

First, let me go on record to say that I think all the *Rocky* movies, including the spinoffs, are great! Second, I think Sylvester Stallone is an underrated actor who only got better as his career progressed. But that's neither here nor there. What's more important is gaining the understanding that careers are not linear. There are several paths to a destination, each of which will have detours. But if you remain flexible in your thinking, you'll remain on the right track.

Have you ever felt stuck? At such moments, no matter what you do to get ahead, something seems to keep you in the same place. You're running, but it's on a treadmill, so you aren't going anywhere. In those moments, it's important to hit pause on the treadmill and step off. Are you learning something while it feels like you're stuck in place? Or are you just expending energy while you turn your proverbial wheels? Are there lessons that will assist you going forward? Are you on the wrong path? Do you need assistance from others? Challenge yourself and your current thinking. If you cannot do it yourself, find a coach or mentor to help you wade through your current place.

But most importantly, remain flexible. Most everyone I know has gotten stuck for a little while, but through reflection, assistance, and guidance, they've found a way out through their flexibility. People who remain truly stuck stay rigidly dedicated to one way forward no matter what—even when that path is blocked. For whatever reason, they cannot consider another way, even with help. If you keep your mind and mentality pliable, you'll find the solution.

So, which Rocky movie are you going to watch first?

Uh, I mean, where do you see a chance to adjust your thinking that might help you move ahead in your career?

IF EVERY CAREER CHOICE YOU'VE MADE HAS BEEN WRONG

Do the opposite. I mean it. That's the advice. Take it!

INSIGHTS

SOMETIMES THE LEADER
ISN'T IN FRONT

You've seen it. There's a chance you may be doing it or experiencing it at this moment. You're on a team, and the "leader" is upfront, proclaiming the bold new direction the business will take. Meanwhile, after the big announcement, everyone in the room looks toward the natural leader, who nods their approval or frowns with displeasure. Leaders come in all shapes and sizes.

Leaders have different styles as well. Many of us are accustomed to leaders being crowned as a result of their title or hierarchy in the organization. However, I've seen many successful leaders take a "servant leadership" approach.

A pastor at my church says there tends to be two types of individuals. The first is the person who walks into the room and says, "Here I am!" The second is the person who walks into the room and says, "There you are!" The servant leader is the latter—focusing their time and energy on the team. They aren't looking for accolades; they just want to achieve the team's goals and help improve the team. Throughout the years, I've been fortunate to work primarily with many servant leaders, and I find them to be incredibly inspiring. These leaders encourage you to make mistakes and will take the time to mentor you when they happen. Why? Because they know mistakes are a vital part of business *and* a real opportunity for significant personal and career development. We don't really progress if we're unable to see, understand, and learn from our mistakes.

This isn't to say that leaders who lead from the front don't have value or aren't true leaders. There are many times when a business or team needs someone to publicly set the direction and vision for the team. And many great leaders can lead from the front or the back of the room. This important thing is to recognize different approaches in ourselves and others.

Take a moment to reflect on what type of leader you are. Is this the leader your team needs? Do they need development or direction? Your answer will help determine the course your team takes.

WHAT WERE YOUR DEVELOPMENT EXPENSES LAST YEAR?

This one is a simple exercise. We all have expense reports that we are required to complete. Many times, we need to do this following a business trip or after attending an industry conference. Go back and review your expenses from this past year. How many of them were focused on your career development? Is there something that needs to change?

Let me begin by saying that we've all seen the "Development Trees" that indicate something along the lines of:

- 70 percent of your development should be on the job

- 20 percent of your development should be from challenging experiences

- 10 percent of your development should be in the classroom

In general, I tend to agree with this breakdown. Still, things get difficult when it's challenging to explain or clearly determine the development I'm getting from my job or experience. If I don't know how I'm developing and progressing, I get frustrated. Most people do. You've probably heard the saying, "People don't leave companies; they leave supervisors." This may be true, but people also decide to leave companies to find more challenging experiences or develop in their careers. People want and need to grow. That's where looking at your expense report can be helpful.

Your expense report is an objective way to assess your development investment. However, it doesn't mean that you didn't experience any development if it turns out that zero dollars were spent on development investment. Many companies have training teams you likely don't have to pay for. Other businesses have job swaps, upskilling programs, or will facilitate conversations with senior leaders to develop team members. These *are* investments, though they may not appear in an expense report. If you've spent nothing on development this year, it may be that nothing needs to change. It may also mean that everything needs to change.

The critical point is that you use the exercise as a reflection opportunity to decide what—if anything—needs to change when it comes to your development investment.

ARE YOU TRYING TO SOLVE A COMPLEX PROBLEM ALONE?

This is one of my favorite anecdotes to share. One day, one of my kids threw a Frisbee onto the roof of our home. At the time, all I had was a mid-sized ladder that, if I stood on the very top, would possibly allow me to hop onto the roof. Before attempting this feat, I realized that even if I managed to get onto the roof, I would still have to find a relatively safe way to lower myself back onto the ladder. There was a gap between the roof and the ladder, and I didn't want to fall 15 feet to the ground, causing myself bodily harm. Looking back at the situation, it should have been reasonably well understood that I needed help. Maybe a neighbor had a taller ladder? Perhaps I could have asked my wife to hold the smaller ladder. There were many options, but I chose *Option Me.*

I felt I could do it on my own, so I proceeded to climb up the insufficiently sized ladder and tried to hop onto the roof of my home. Sometime between my first and second hop, I realized how hilarious I must've looked to passersby! I did not possess the proper equipment to do it on my own, yet there I was, trying to be a hero. I was fortunate that I didn't hurt myself. Unable to get on to the roof, I eventually called a neighbor who brought a longer ladder. With help, I was quickly able to secure the Frisbee and remove it from the roof.

We often approach challenges in our careers the *very same way*.

How often have you been asked to complete an assignment only to realize that you had no idea where to begin? That realization—and we've all had it—may be one of the first signs that it might be better not to attempt a journey alone. We've all heard the phrase, "Two heads are better than one." Many times, two people looking at the same problem come to different solutions. Now imagine three or four people looking at the same problem, and you can quickly see how inviting more colleagues into your problem might assist you in creating a viable solution. In high school, when we took a test, we were penalized if we looked at someone else's answers. In college, it was the same, but at times we had to complete challenges as a group. Somewhere along the way, we thought we'd receive extra credit for solving work problems independently. Reality is typically the opposite.

What problem have you been trying to solve on your own? Who can help you find the solution?

THE BEST PERSON TO MAKE *YOU-TIME*? YOU.

Have you ever read an e-mail from your boss and gotten frustrated because they keep giving you more work to do—*or, ahem, is that just me?* Seriously, it's almost like I'm *at work* or something.

The reality of life is that many of us have to work to earn a living. We need the money from our job to pay for school, clothes, transportation, food, and many other necessities. We work to earn money. We're not showing up for fun, even when we're passionate about our job. So, it's not odd at all when our boss gives us more work to do. *However, it is* odd to wait for our boss to let us know when it's the right time to take a break from work. I know too many people who wait for a sign from their boss that it's the right time to take a vacation or break from work. Is it really in your boss' interest to tell you when to take time off?

The great thing about being human is that we're all different. Even siblings with the same parents have unique qualities that set them apart from one another. This reality plays out at work as well. Two employees on the same team, with very similar backgrounds and skills, can operate very differently—especially when it comes to how they approach vacation time. People have different needs and priorities. In the end, the best person to tell you when to take a break is the person looking back at you in the mirror every morning. Ever wake up in the morning and dread the day ahead? It might be time to take a break!

Your manager could be the best manager ever, and still have no idea of the perfect time for you to take a break. It's personal. Now, if you're reading this, I'll caution you if you suddenly think, "He's right! I need a break tomorrow!" Most of us only get so much vacation or paid time off each year, so it's best to use it wisely. The point is to make it work for *you*. I know a senior leader who, if stressed, will use his time off to go see a movie on a random afternoon. It works for him. That might not be how everyone unwinds.

Recently, there have been a lot of articles about people waking up and realizing the job they're in is not the job they want to be in, so they make a switch—many of them immediately. To me, the Great Resignation seemed to be a global inflection point; we all suddenly felt compelled to reflect on who we wanted to be when we grow up and if we were on the right track to become that person. Whether we were furloughed in our jobs, our jobs terminated, or simply contacted by a recruiter to determine our level of interest in taking a new role, the Great Resignation became a big *you-time* moment.

But there are lots of ways to catch your breath. Sometimes we need a major change; other times, we just need to pause and reflect on our journey.

Not sure if it's the right time for you-time? Think of the moment as a metaphorical *pause* button on your career and life. When the story of your life and career start to feel like they're fast-forwarding without you, it might be time to hit the pause button.

THE BEST WAY TO DETERMINE YOUR CAREER WORTH

The concept of supply and demand can apply to your career. When I speak to a group of professionals, I often ask them open-ended questions. One of my favorite things to ask is, "What is your career worth today?" I receive many excellent responses, but the most basic and common answer to the question is, "The market." In other words, the market determines a person's career worth.

You may feel you are worth $200,000 in annual salary, but unless you're able to find an employer willing to pay it, that's not your worth. A lot of people tell me that their company determines their worth. There is some truth to that statement. A company does represent a part of the market. But your company is *not the entire market*. If you believe that you're worth $20,000 more than what your company is paying you, your company either agrees with you or they don't. If they agree with you, congratulations, you're likely to get a salary increase! What happens if they disagree with you?

The space between what you think you're worth and what your company thinks you're worth is an opportunity. As a coach, I spend a lot of time talking to people about that "worth gap." I don't generally sugarcoat things when I'm coaching people. So, if they tell me they're worth $20,000 more than their company is paying them, I ask them how they know. They can give me many answers, and pull data from websites and comparison platforms, but unless the answer is, "I have an offer in my hand right now from another company for $20,000 more than I'm making," their statement is pure fiction. That doesn't mean it *couldn't* be true or that there isn't potential. It just means that at a particular moment in time, it's not true.

My approach can feel harsh, but if you read my first book, you've understood this to be "par for the course" with me. I challenge people to be honest with themselves and with me. If I take that approach, it doesn't mean I lack faith in you. It just means I don't think you've taken the steps to truly understand your career market value.

If the market determines your career value, then it's the market you must test your value against. Some people think I'm asking them to leave their company when I give them this advice. While it may seem that way, what I really want is for people to understand there are options. When people are unhappy with their pay or the opportunities afforded to them within a company, it's a common instinct to blame the company. We all feel trapped at times, but I try to dispel the perception that we're not in control of our careers. I want people to embrace the idea that the market has many opportunities—should they wish to pursue them.

If you apply for ten jobs and receive no interviews, do you feel better or worse about your current position? Do you have a better or worse understanding of your career market value? If you apply for ten jobs and receive three offers—all at $20,000 or more than what you are making today—do you have a better or worse understanding of your career market value?

When it comes to your career value, "When in doubt, find out!" What you do with that information is up to you.

CAREER ADVICE I WOULD GIVE MY YOUNGER SELF

Once, I had an employer that asked an open-ended question on LinkedIn: What career advice would you give your younger self? Typically, I give questions like these very little thought. My general disposition in life isn't to look backward. I try to make decisions in real-time, hoping that this approach will prevent me from looking back one day look back only to regret the things I didn't try or do. As a result, whenever I'm asked this type of question, my initial response is that I wouldn't change a thing and I'd tell myself to just keep going. I've made good and not-so-good decisions, but I don't regret things that have gotten me to where I am today. I stand by that response, generally.

But on that particular day, the question landed a bit differently. Instead of interpreting the question as a prompt to detail what I'd advise myself to avoid or change, I decided to answer it with what I would reinforce. With that lens, here's the career advice I would give my younger self:

- Know and protect your brand

- Soar with your strengths

- Leverage your network

- Have someone who will give you honest feedback

Are you the hardest worker? Are you the most knowledgeable? Are you liked by all? Are you a procrastinator? These are perceptions other people will have about you in your career. Now we don't always get to control all aspects of our brand, but we do get to manage a lot of areas. Are you gracious with your time? Are you quick to say "thanks" to those who assist you? Who is it that you want to be in your career? Go live it!

In terms of strengths, we all have them. How are you maximizing them? There is a field of business philosophy that suggests that instead of trying to minimize the things you don't naturally do well, focus your time on expanding the areas in which you naturally excel. I believe in that perspective. I've seen it play out positively on many different occasions. I encourage people to meditate on what they are good at and to use it to their advantage in their careers as soon as they realize what it is.

The idea of six degrees of separation came from an experiment. The idea was to keep sending postcards until they reached their intended destination. On average, it took between five and six sends, and thus the degrees of separation between people were understood. A separate experiment was done to understand if job seekers were more likely to find a new job from people they knew or didn't know. As I recall, the overwhelming evidence was that we're more likely to land jobs from people we don't already know. That's because *new information, new opportunities* come from *new* people. What should we take from this? Expand your network. Talk to people in your network and ask them to connect you with someone new. Before you know it, six degrees of separation will only be one or two and then, look out!

Finally, have someone that will tell you the truth. It's interesting reading some of the stories of people who became famous but still have a couple of childhood friends in their lives. Or still listen to their parents or close loved ones. Sometimes the biggest obstacle to ongoing success is early success. We start to believe we did it on our own or that we're better than we think. Having a constant in your career who can give you an honest answer is vital to growth. I encourage all of you to have at least one person like this.

Good luck, younger me!

WORDS DO MATTER

In sports, in the heat of the moment, it's easy to lose your cool and say something that can get you kicked out of the game, off the team, or in the penalty box for a few minutes. Careers are the same. Being successful at work requires that we manage many things happening at once, and that often includes *what we say* as well as what *people say to us.*

If your team is working on a project and two peers begin to challenge one another, it can lead to a better outcome. Why? Because they are looking at the problem from different angles. However, if your perspective is the one being challenged, or a person's feedback seems directed *at you,* things may feel a little personal. If it feels like a person has an agenda against you, then it's common to feel like you are forced to defend yourself or your position. In these moments, it becomes essential to know who you are and what you are there to do.

I bring up the sports analogy because I see many similarities between sports and work. You and your co-workers are on a team. You're competing to achieve a common goal. There's an opponent—be it time or resources. In the heat of the battle, it's easy to lose your cool. That's when it's important to understand the things that get you riled up and have a plan for them. There are so many scenarios that could play out; there are too many to list. That said, whatever they are, there's a good chance you've seen them before. Maybe someone talks politics, or tells inappropriate jokes, or asks questions for the sake of asking, and, and, and . . . so many things trigger us at work. I'm here to tell you that unless it's your company, let it go. Even if it is your company, you may want to let it go for another day.

When you find yourself reaching a point of frustration, remember who you are and why you're there. Take a deep breath, go to your happy place, remember you're on the same team (even if it doesn't feel like it), assume positive intent, determine if the juice is worth the squeeze, and sail on. You can't control what other people say or do, but you can control your own approach.

Ahh! Now, doesn't that feel better?

IT'S EASIER TO BLAME

In elementary school, I remember being told that if someone was pointing at me, a clever thing to say was: "You have one finger pointing at me, but there are three more are pointing back at you!" It's more than just a clever punch line for an eight-year-old; it's a way of thinking about difficult situations. I see this in career discussions quite a bit.

- "My manager isn't supporting me."
- "One of my peers has the same job I do, but I'm assessed differently."
- "That person has it easier than I do."
- "Our business would succeed if that group over there was better at their jobs."

There are several different scenarios in which we rush to apply blame. It's harder for us to remember that, at the end of the day, it's rarely someone else's fault if we're not where we want to be in our career. It's easier to point the finger at others and highlight how *they're* failing. It's much harder to look inward and figure out what you could have done differently. And it may be the key to finding success.

It's certainly possible that any of the scenarios I've listed above are true. However, when we succumb to the idea that our ability to achieve our goals rests in the hands of others, we take a big step backward in owning our careers. One premise I'll sometimes see in these situations is that the aggrieved person often feels that the situation isn't "fair." The concept of *fairness* is difficult to address because what is fair to one person may not be to another. It also implies that something is owed to a person if things are out of balance. There is a scene in one of my favorite movie series, *Rocky*, where Rocky is talking to his son about life. He explains that life is challenging and we all get knocked down, but the point is how many times you get up after life knocks you down. In other words, take accountability for what you can control, no matter the circumstance. I believe this message applies both inside and outside of work.

Now for the tricky part. Can you name which Rocky movie I'm referencing?

YOU DON'T *HAVE TO* HAVE FUN AT WORK–BUT IT'S FUNNER IF YOU DO!

Isn't this the truth? Maybe I've just been lucky in my career, but I've met some *seriously* funny people at work. Some of my co-workers would have to do a lot to prove to me that they aren't moonlighting as comedians in their free time! I'm always amazed by the person who can perfectly capture the current situation in a witty summation. Other times, I'm left overcome by laughter because a work question led to a smirk or grimace on someone's face and the person's true feelings were clear, if even for a split second, and it brought a moment of humor to the situation. Whatever it is, it is okay to have fun at work!

Show me the boss who says work can't be fun, and I'll show you the boss with a lot of turnover on their team. Now, if you're like me, you are actively working through the types of jobs where it might not be okay to have fun on the job. For example, police officers, judges, CIA operatives, FBI agents, corrections officers, and airplane pilots may not have the type of job that leaves a lot of room for fun every day. While that may be true, my guess is there are still times and situations in those jobs when it's okay to have a little fun.

Across your life, you'll spend a significant amount of time at work. Let's say you work between the ages of eighteen and sixty-four, for an average of eight hours a day. In your lifetime, you'll spend just under 100,000 hours at work. The total is even greater if you start working before you're eighteen and continue working past sixty-four. The point is if you spend that much time of your life working, make it fun! Find a job you love. Find people you love working with. Find both, and the time you spend at work will fly by.

I love what I do and the people I work with; that combination has proven to be valuable for me throughout my career. Don't fret if you haven't experienced that feeling yet. Like I say in my book *You're Worth It! Navigating Your Career in Corporate America:* You are in charge of your career. You are the captain of the ship. You are—and should be—in the driver's seat when it comes to your career. You are the lead actor on the career stage. If you don't like the director, producer, or co-stars, it might be time to exit stage left.

IF I HAD AN HOUR

There are many quotes attributed to Albert Einstein, but there's one I've always loved: "If I had an **hour to solve a problem**, I'd spend fifty-five minutes thinking about the **problem** and five minutes thinking about solutions."

Before we jump into trying to solve anything, it's important to understand the problem. This advice is often given to salespeople. When trying to solve a customer's problem, make sure you're listening to the problem so you can determine the root cause. I'm sure doctors must come across this all the time as well. We go into the doctor's office having read about our symptoms online, so we're really only there for the doctor to sign off on our own medical advice. Yet, every time you go to see the doctor, they check your pulse and weight, right? They ask you a bunch of questions. They listen for the responses. Why? Because they are trained to understand that while their patients have the best intentions and own self-interest in mind, understanding the solution means not jumping to conclusions. Instead, they utilize tried and true methods to compare your symptoms, assess vital signs, and compare your responses against the mountain of research completed in their respective medical field. In other words, before diagnosing you, they are trying to understand the depth and breadth of the problem. That is not only sage medical practice, but also great career advice!

Let's look at a scenario. You are presented with two jobs. One of the jobs is the next logical step in your career, pays more money, leads a bigger team, and you wouldn't have to relocate. The other job would also give you a salary bump, but is in a different location, and your path afterward is less clear. Which position do you take? On the surface, it seems pretty straightforward. The first job seems to have everything you would want with the least amount of life disruption. However, what if the second job gave you a better understanding of how the business was run? What if the second job checked the box on a critical requirement for a job you want to be in five years? What if the second job was the same pay, but in another country? Do these scenarios change your response? Should they?

When problems arise at work, it can be easy to believe they are the same as problems you've faced in the past—and they might be. However, taking the time to reflect, to get differing or varying opinions, and to consider viable alternatives before establishing a clear path forward, can save you time, money, and effort in the long run.

If you had taken an hour to think about a problem you had today, would you have arrived at a different solution or conclusion?

IF YOU HAD A CHANCE TO DO IT ALL OVER AGAIN

At a fundraising event for a successful charity that helps people who have previously been homeless furnish their new homes cheaply but in a dignified manner, the charity's founder said something that really got my attention. He shared that his idea for the charity started when he was nearly sixty years old. He started his most meaningful career *after* he retired from his first career. His words shattered my thinking on conventional careers. What would you do if you had the chance to do it all again? Before I'd heard this founder speak, I thought, "It's impossible to start over again, so what's the point of asking this question?" After hearing his story, my perspective changed. My thoughts evolved into, "What are you waiting for? If there is something you would do differently in your career, start today! If you want an Act Two or Act Three, it's not too late."

Have you wanted to be a musician? Did you want to open a bakery shop? Have you dreamed of working in Human Resources? Okay, maybe I took it too far with that last example, but the point is that it's never too late. Sometimes, we look for reasons to avoid change or put off our passions and dreams. When we take that approach, we don't have to look too far for excuses. There are many reasons to keep doing things the way we've always done them. Maybe it's security. Indeed, it's scary to go from a steady-paying job to a passion project that might not provide regular income. Maybe you have a family to think about. How will going back to school work out if you also have to ensure that everyone gets where they need to go on time? These are rational thoughts when thinking about a significant change. However, it's important to know that you are not alone. You'll see the most notable acts of kindness from the most unexpected places if you simply invite others on your journey.

A story I tell quite a bit is how I was able to publish my first book. First the dream. Since I was a child, I have always wanted to write a book. I loved reading Stephen King; his books made me think that one day I'd write a book worth reading. Fast forward, I'm nearly thirty years into my career, married, with two kids, a demanding job, and coaching youth sports when I decide, "Now is when I want to write my first book!" Once I made the decision, and decided to tell other people about it, their encouragement meant so much to me. The actual writing process became a passion project. How did I get it done? I traveled a lot, so I found free time at hotels, on planes, before bed. I wanted to find the time, so I did. Once I finished the manuscript, I wanted to publish it but had no idea where to begin. That's when I enlisted my colleagues on LinkedIn. I published an article asking for help on publishing a manuscript, and within two weeks, I had dozens of leads. I followed up on each one. I'm happy to tell you, they led to my first book being published and sold everywhere books are sold! I was officially an author. All it took was follow-through and help from my friends.

Want to start over? How about starting now? What could you accomplish if you put your mind to it?

LEADERS CAN LIGHT FIRES OR PUT THEM OUT

Close your eyes. Think about the best leader you've ever worked for. What are some of their most significant characteristics? What made them "the best?" Did they say the right words at the right time? Did they develop you so that you would go on to do bigger and better things? Did they challenge you to find the best version of yourself? Did they open doors for you? Did they remove barriers? Great leaders can make you feel as if you can conquer the world. Sometimes these leaders believe in you more than you believe in yourself. They allow you to flourish by harnessing gifts and abilities that you may not have known were within you.

Now, what if *you* had the potential to be that leader?

You've reflected on that *great leader*, the one from your past who made such an impact on you. Tell me, what's stopping you from being that type of leader as well? Are you able to do those same things and influence people around you? Are there others, maybe peers or colleagues early in their careers, who would benefit from someone lighting a spark within them that would help *them* become a great leader? What keeps you from taking that step, making the introduction, reaching out to your team, peers, or people on other teams to tell them that you see the fantastic leader they are becoming?

You'd be surprised to learn how many leaders there are out there who *should* have every reason to be confident. People whose expertise, skills, and history of performance make them remarkable, but they lack confidence because their spark has been dimmed by a supervisor, peer, or senior leader. In such situations, that leader needs someone to help revive their energy. They need someone who sees them for who they are *and* who they are capable of being. In short, they likely require you to intervene. They need you to get involved in their career. It may be uncomfortable at first, but it will become easier over time.

They say it takes a village to raise a child. The concept also applies to developing influential leaders with successful careers.

Careerwise, be a fire starter!

THE MORE QUESTIONS I ASK, THE MORE I'M PREPARED

True story. I had a supervisor ask me to take the lead on a big project. There were multiple aspects to the project. It was global, had several key stakeholders, numerous workstreams, and several key milestones. In addition, it had a significant impact on the organization's profits. As a result, I asked many questions to better understand the scope and define my approach. After about five minutes, I could tell my supervisor was getting slightly annoyed. At the time, I wasn't sure what was annoying them, but I did find out eventually. The supervisor felt that asking so many questions upfront meant I wasn't committed to the project or trying to convince myself it was a good project. The truth was that I was genuinely scoping the project. I was trying to understand as much as I could upfront to ascertain the project's boundaries and define what success looked like. It was my way of preparing for the journey ahead. In my mind, it was simple—the more questions I asked, the better prepared I would be.

One of the best lessons I've learned from other successful leaders is how to listen and how to ask questions. There is an oft-used example shared among sales teams that I'll mention. There's an eager salesperson who is asked to grow sales for their company. The first thing they do is meet with a potential customer to tell them about the many ways their products can help the customer grow their business. Instead of starting by listening to the customer, they dove directly into creating solutions. Of course, the salesperson missed several opportunities to understand the real challenge faced by the customer, and as a result, they also missed opportunities to increase sales.

In contrast, another salesperson with the same goal sets up a meeting with a customer. At the customer meeting, they sought to understand the customer's challenges. They asked clarifying questions to ensure they knew what problems they were trying to solve. In the end, they engaged the right network to create a customized solution for the customer and grew the business significantly over established goals.

The point is that when we're trying to solve a problem, it's a good habit to start by asking questions, seeking to understand, and listening. How would you apply this concept in your job today?

YOU DON'T NEED TO BURN BRIDGES TO WIN. BUILD THEM INSTEAD.

Maybe it's sports culture. Potentially it's politics. It's possible that it's been bred in our homes. Somewhere along the way, we've been taught that for someone to win, someone else must lose. We see this all the time in negotiating. You go to a flea market and see the listed price. You find something you want, and immediately you begin to haggle with the vendor to reduce the cost. You're successful and walk away feeling that you won a great bargain. It could be the margins were so big that the vendor still won the negotiation. Or it could be that the vendor sold the item for cost or even under the price just to keep food on the table. Either way, this mentality frequently crops up in work situations.

I previously worked at a company where a large group of individuals started at one time. We were a cohort of about thirty new hires from all over the country, and all of us started simultaneously. Over the years, we all kept tabs on one another.

If one of us was promoted faster than the others, we were happy for them, but it also meant the rest of us were falling behind. Usually, most of us earned promotions every two to three years. If someone wasn't promoted after three years, we secretly wondered what was wrong with them or if they would be leaving the company soon. Now, to be fair, the company did promote this cut-throat culture through its various traditions. I didn't realize it at the time, but it created personal stress. I wondered if I was truly happy for my colleagues. If I saw someone else promoted, I knew it meant they were making more money which, in turn, made me want more money. If I fell too far behind, was everyone wondering how long I would be at the company? Was I the person to pity? It took me a long time before I understood that everyone could win.

Sure, in sports, there is typically a winner and a loser, but a perspective I had never considered was that everyone participating was a winner. I can hear you groan at this moment. You're thinking, "He's one of those people that thinks everyone should get a participation ribbon!" I can assure you that when it comes to sports, I'm perfectly fine with a winner and a loser. However, what often gets missed is sportsmanship. At the end of the game, it's typical for the two teams to come together and shake hands or acknowledge a game well-played. In that sense, everyone is winning simply by striving to win. It's *this mentality* that I believe needs to translate to our careers.

When I stopped looking at my peers as competitors, I became truly happy for their success. Then, a funny thing happened—I felt less stress in my life. I was happier. I still wanted to win, but not at the expense of a friendship. If I had information that could help them get promoted, I shared it. Eventually, they did the same. Winning in your career does not need to come at someone else's expense. Burning bridges eventually leaves you completely alone. Building bridges creates a path to success that you may not have even imagined.

It's not too late to put down the metaphorical flamethrower and pick up a hammer. Where will you build your bridges?

YOU'RE GENERALLY ONLY AS GOOD AS YOUR LAST SUCCESS

Have you ever been part of a company or business that's fired someone who had been—at one point—very successful in their job? We all like to sensationalize that maybe they were fired for some illicit act or some gossip-worthy reason. However, it's been my experience that these once-great individuals are often fired because they were no longer successful. They had been riding the wave of previous successes for years, and their supervisor realized they were no longer the valuable employee they used to be. You've probably heard the following phrase: "The greatest obstacle to future success is past success." I have found this to be true time and again.

My favorite group to observe at work is the sales team. This group of individuals fascinates me because they have to hunt to find and grow their business. If they don't close the deal, they don't get paid. There is no more transparent way to run an organization than to promote, "If you don't win, we don't pay you." The sales team, however, takes risks on themselves. They are betting that they will achieve their goals. They are betting on themselves. The reward for taking on this risk? More money. Often, these individuals can earn a significant amount of money each year by making more for the company. Salespeople are the ultimate example of "You're only as good as your last success." But what about the rest of us?

How does this principle apply to the rest of the organization? Many functions in companies are paid whether or not they've had a hand in closing a deal. How are people in accounting, finance, human resources, IT, or another functional area treated when they aren't winning? The concept is very similar. Many organizations require that every employee have quarterly, semi-annual, or annual goals. Those goals are usually something that can be measured. If you are part of the accounting team, and you found a significant error that saved the company millions, there's a good chance you will have a great year financially. Suppose you are the HR professional who terminated the employee that created a financial risk for the company through their questionable practices. In that case, you, too, may be looking at a good year ahead financially. But what happens when those same individuals are satisfied with their efforts for that year and don't continue to look for ways to improve? The following year they don't achieve their stated goals. Usually, this will result in a performance improvement plan. If they don't achieve their goals the next year, there's an increased likelihood that they could be at risk of termination. Some companies are faster and more aggressive in their practices when employees haven't attained their goals.

We must push for continuous improvement to sustain continued success in our careers. Not doing so puts us at risk of fewer financial benefits and even potentially losing our jobs. We'd all do well to remember that we're only as good as our last win. Celebrate success. Pat yourself on the back. Then find the next victory. Where is yours?

ENJOY THE STOPS

How many of you have been in a hurry to climb the top of the career mountain as fast as you can? If that's you, raise your hand. Many of us are competitive by nature. We can't help it. We've been raised to try to win whatever game we're playing. I've spoken with many leaders who had the first ten to fifteen years of their careers mapped out. They knew when or if they were going to have kids. They knew when they would get promoted. They were willing to sacrifice their weekends and personal lives to reach their intended destinations. Many people I know who have taken this approach have indeed achieved their goals. If that's who you want to be, I applaud you. I also have a word of caution for you.

In speaking with leaders who have taken such a focused approach, there's an intriguing commonality that I've noticed. Almost all of them have regretted some aspect of their past. It could have been the personal relationship that ended due to a move, or an opportunity to take another job that they declined because it didn't fit into the plan. Sometimes, when these leaders finally arrived at the mountaintop, they realized they weren't as happy as they thought they would be.

I'm not trying to say that going after your dreams isn't a worthy goal. The concept I'm trying to convey here is that going after your dreams at all costs *usually does have a price*. A key concept in business is *opportunity cost*. Said simply, it's what you give up by pursuing an opportunity. If I have two job offers, choosing one means I give up the other. The opportunity cost is the job I didn't choose. If I'm in a relationship and I choose to relocate for a job, and it causes my relationship to end, then the opportunity cost is the relationship.

As much as we might want them to be, career paths are rarely straight. Usually, they are quite windy. And that's what I love about them. I have a lot of HR colleagues, and I can't think of a single one who came to HR the same way. They all had different routes to their HR destination. Heck, HR may not be their final destination. If you have the perspective that careers are windy *and long*, then you can start to appreciate the many stops along the way.

When I was young, my dad would take us on long trips. We visited the Grand Canyon. We went to Pikes Peak. I used to think the destinations were the best part. The car rides were so long that I couldn't wait to get to wherever we were going. Later in life, I realized the car rides were the best parts. Hanging out with my brothers. Singing songs together. Laughing at whatever jokes we told to fill the time. I've even come to appreciate those annoying moments when someone was "sitting too close to me." The trips weren't special because of where we went. They were special because of the people with whom the trips were taken.

As I've progressed at work, I've realized this perspective also applies to careers.

By all means, chase your dreams! If it's important to you, focus on a plan you can achieve quickly. However, you'd do well to remember that while the destination can be a wonderful place, there is beauty in the journey.

Is it time for you to stop, look around, and enjoy the moment?

WIN OR LEARN

One of my favorite movies to watch when I want to genuinely laugh out loud is *Talladega Nights*. The movie follows the racing career of Ricky Bobby, who has won a lot of races throughout his career. One of the lines he learned from his father is, "If you ain't first, you're last." While that line is an absolute classic, and truly hilarious, it's terrible career advice! If we went through our careers believing that we were losers if we didn't consistently win, we'd be quite unhappy in life! A better piece of advice was shared with me early in my career: "In every situation throughout your career, win or learn."

Win or learn. That concept applies to nearly every aspect of life, but it's one I particularly like to use as a basketball coach. In any sport, teams can spend a lot of time preparing for their opponent. They spend time learning the plays, running to get in shape, working together as a team, and maybe even watching training or strategy films—all to prepare for a game. When the game comes around, both teams play admirably, and perhaps the game is won or lost on a last-second shot. One team is filled with joy. The other team is left to wonder where it went wrong. Let's be clear: I don't think many of us like to lose. Losing isn't fun. But I think it's wrong to assume that a "loss" is the only result. It doesn't have to be. Losing can be the beginning of learning.

There are some themes I've observed about practices when my teams have won or lost a few games in a row. When a team is on a winning streak, they're happy because they've won a few games and look forward to winning again. After several wins, practices can be different. Sometimes the players goof off, don't completely listen, or don't try as hard. Success has often softened their focus. But losing, well, few things sharpen a player's focus a much as a loss. Teams that are hungry for a win will eat up every word a coach says. They'll work harder. They'll run faster. Essentially, they become better learners because they don't want to continue losing.

Do you see parallels with your career? Whenever you are in a situation that feels like an "L" instead of that coveted "W" that's earned by a win, it's essential to take time to reflect. If there are people you trust, it can lead to significant breakthroughs to ask them to assist in that reflection. Ask yourself what you could have done differently. What went wrong? Was the loss avoidable, and if so, how?

In other words, learn. When it comes to your career, if you didn't win, what did you learn?

TIMING IS EVERYTHING, SO BUILD A GOOD WATCH

Have you ever met someone who always seems to be at the right place at the right time? And I'm mostly kidding here, but let's be real, none of us can stand these people. From afar, it looks like everything they do is successful. They seem to get the promotion that maybe you always wanted. They certainly get promoted faster than everyone else. They get the amazing projects. Their background is the same as yours, but a certain high-powered leader took a liking to them and helped them. In short, it's like they are wearing a watch that tells them when and where to be for a win. We have a love-hate relationship with these people because we envy them. They appear to have something we don't, and it's something special. However, I've found that not everything is as it seems. Many of these individuals worked hard *to create* the opportunities they've been afforded. They weren't given some magical watch that told them when something would happen for them; instead, they worked hard and built their own watch.

Let's break this one down further. Have you ever read stories about billionaires like Bill Gates, Jeff Bezos, Oprah Winfrey, or Sheryl Sandberg? We like to attribute success in life to the amount of money a person has. While I don't subscribe to that line of thinking, I do think there are some common attributes shared by successful people. Let's look at Bill Gates. Yes, he built an empire called Microsoft. He also spent countless hours early in his career learning his craft and creating a vision. Okay, let's turn to Oprah—successful television show, cable channel, book club, and magazine. We assume it's been easy for her. She turned one success into other successes, right? It's easy to miss that she had a vision for her future that meant stepping away from the type of television shows that were popular at the time and paving a new path forward. Many of us miss the relentless determination and savvy business moves of self-made billionaires. On the outside, their way to prosperity seems inevitable, but when we think of it that way, we're missing the complete picture. The final image isn't everything; it doesn't capture the preparation and work that led to what we're used to seeing.

Successful people plan for the future. The Oprahs, Bills, Jeffs, and Sheryls of the world saw a future no one else did and worked tirelessly to realize it. In other words, they were in the right place at the right time *because* they built the place and the time. They had a good watch to follow because they made the watch. Think about the most insane career goal you would like to accomplish. See it? What would it take for you to attain it? What would you have to sacrifice? What would you need to do differently? What would you need to risk? What would you need to change right now?

What are you waiting for? The clock is ticking.

BEING POLITE IS A GREAT CAREER MOVE

If you're like me, you grew up watching *SportsCenter*. It's a show on ESPN that captures sports highlights from around the world. Because it condenses the day's highlights, it's a huge time saver and lets you focus on the most relevant points. The show did a great episode that focused on a particular issue from an era of baseball. If you are a fan of baseball, you've heard of the Steroid Era—it's when multiple players were accused of using steroids to improve their performance. One of the main players in the Steroid Era was a fantastic hitter named Barry Bonds. Toward the end of his career, he sometimes hit the ball so far that it landed in the water behind San Francisco's ballpark. If you were to look at the totality of his career, you would think that he would have entered the Hall of Fame the moment he was eligible. But today, he is still not in the Baseball Hall of Fame. Another player on the scene at the tail end of the Steroid Era was David Ortiz. He also had some amazing feats, but there were always questions whether his success was influenced by steroids. He, however, did end up getting into the Baseball Hall of Fame. What was the difference?

Many fans and people in the media perceived Barry Bonds as ungracious and anti-social. During interviews, he was often short with the media. The perception was that maybe he wasn't the nicest person. On the other hand, David Ortiz was perceived as quite the opposite. He joked with the media. He gave funny responses. He appeared to be more sociable. I have no idea whether David Ortiz was nicer than Barry Bonds. But their personal brands at work were different. People perceived them as complete opposites—one was open and fun, the other closed and serious. Any ideas why one got into the Baseball Hall of Fame and the other did not?

Now to be fair, I am not a baseball writer, and they ultimately determine who gets in and who does not. So, it is fair to say that I may be oversimplifying the situation. Still, I've seen the same situation play out repeatedly—the more likable employee seems to have more success in their career. It turns out that *please* and *thank you* are also essential throughout our careers. If two qualified leaders are up for a promotion, it usually goes to the person others believe they would enjoy working around more. If two people on a team make a mistake, the manager usually gives a little more leeway to the employee everyone likes. I'm not judging the situation. I'm not telling you it's right, I'm telling you that it happens. How you treat people at work matters. How nice you are to other people at work impacts your career.

This quote attributed to Carolyn Flack is one of my favorites: "In a world where you can be anything, be kind." Doesn't that sum it up? If you take nothing else from this book, I want you to walk away with the idea that we live in a world that seems to promote division, but we don't have to follow that lead. This world emphasizes our differences and almost encourages meanness. Kindness is not rare—it's just not highlighted as much. It's not as newsworthy.

Change it! Bring kindness to your career as a way to spread it to the world!

***EVERYONE* IS IMPORTANT IN A SUCCESSFUL BUSINESS**

Do your actions reflect this? I remember getting a certification in Strategic Workforce Planning—the concept of taking a company's vision and understanding the people implications of it. During the course, one of the company examples they give was Disney. They analyzed the entire company and found that of all the positions across the company, one of the most important roles was the sweeper at the theme parks. Why would the sweepers be as crucial as some of the executives? Well, it turns out that they understand they are in the business of providing great experiences. The sweepers are trained to assist whenever something goes wrong at their parks. Not sure where to go? Ask a sweeper. A crying child who has lost their parents will likely approach one of the friendly sweepers. They are the glue that holds the wonderful experience together. Disney figured that out early and is still a wildly successful company after nearly one hundred years of being in business. In a nutshell, companies that are winning consistently understand that everyone is important.

I've been fortunate to work in some of the most prominent companies in the world. Their financial success over the years has been consistent. When I took a step back to think of how they've accomplished this feat, several thoughts come to mind. First, they have commonalities in their cultures. Each company has a culture that is reflected throughout the entire organization. Second, they hire good people. When it comes down to it, good things happen when you hire good people. Third, and maybe the most important commonality such companies share, is that they all seem to value every single person in the company. Hierarchy doesn't lead to a person's value; rather, all employees are valuable.

At three of the very successful companies I was a part of, I saw the CEO meet and speak with employees at every level of the organization. They made time for lunches with staff or would show up unannounced at business meetings. But it wasn't just the CEO. Senior leaders in those organizations made a point to connect with all employees—as best they could. They made each employee feel special. Magic happens when employees feel valued. We all know that engaged employees are more productive. Countless surveys and studies prove that fact. Each year companies survey their employees to assess their engagement. Why? Because they know it matters to the bottom line.

Where is your company in terms of valuing <u>every</u> employee? What role do you play?

THE BEST-LAID PLANS OFTEN FAIL. ADAPT.

What is the famous line from Charles Darwin? "It is not the strongest of the species that survives, nor the most intelligent; it is the one most adaptable to change." We see this every day, don't we? One movie I enjoy watching is called *Tin Cup*. It stars Kevin Costner, and he plays a golfer that is on the verge of success. In one of the movie's scenes, he leads the other golfers and comes to a critical hole. He can go for the win, but there is a risk the ball will go in the water. There were other options, but he wanted to win—we've all been there. He hits the shot, and the ball goes into the water. Instead of adjusting his strategy, he tries the same shot again. The same result happens several times. Ultimately, because he stubbornly stuck to his plan and didn't adapt, he's at risk of qualifying for future tournaments. It's a great example of what happens when we can't move past something or adapt to reality.

I read an article that focused on the "Great Recession" of 2008. It analyzed the companies that effectively navigated through—and out—of the recession against those that did not.

The themes were striking. At the onset of recession, all the companies knew that difficult times were coming; however, there were differences in how the companies responded. The companies that performed well immediately came up with a Plan B and a Plan C. They were able to quickly pivot their strategies and adjust to the day's reality. The companies that fared poorly kept their original strategy, hoping that the situation around them would change. In other words, instead of changing, these companies waited for the world to change around them. The companies that were most adaptable to change made it through the proverbial storm. And what are companies? A collection of people. The people, the leaders within the companies needed to change. They either did or they didn't.

Some people are lucky enough to work for the same company their entire career. When I get the chance to talk to the few people I know who have done this, they tell a similar story: The company had its ups and downs, but I changed in this way, or I changed in that way as the environment changed. They evolved to the current atmosphere. There's a saying attributed to Benjamin Franklin, "Nothing is certain except death and taxes." While true, I would add the words "and change." Change is a certainty. In the journey that is our career, we'd all be wise to look for the signs ahead. If there's a curve in the road, be prepared to adjust your course accordingly. Not doing so will likely lead to a crash.

One of the greatest martial artists to perform, Bruce Lee, described his fighting style as being like "water." Water adapts to its environment. You put it in a cup, and it takes the shape the cup. You put it on a flat surface, and it spreads out. He encouraged his students to "be like water." It's excellent advice for your career as well.

Now, who's thirsty?

MEANINGFUL DEVELOPMENT USUALLY INVOLVES RISK

As you read this, I imagine you telling me, "Easy for you to advise about risk; it's my career, not yours!" And you're right. But, let's start with the obvious: Can you have worthwhile career development *without* taking a risk? I would answer the question with an emphatic, "Yes." I've worked with quite a few leaders who took the next logical step in their careers and saw significant development. Often, things progressed because of their supervisors. In those situations, the next step was logical, people knew what they were walking into, they were supported, and while I'm sure there was a fraction of risk, it generally did not keep them up at night. They weren't left wondering if they had made the right decision. There's a time and place for the safe approach. However, whenever I've asked senior leaders what positions helped truly propel their careers, they inevitably share stories about making career decisions involving some level of risk. Invariably, the most remarkable growth often results from risk.

So, what is risk? At some level, every decision we make in our career has an *opportunity cost*. When we make one choice, we give up something else. For example, if I decide to work for one company, it typically means that I can't work for a different one. The opportunity cost was the other company. On a grander scale, if I have the option between getting promoted on my same career path or starting a bakery, there is a significant opportunity cost to pursuing the bakery—or what I could call a *career risk*. There are many angles of risk in such a decision. Deciding to open a bakery might mean less financial freedom. It might mean an inconsistent revenue stream. Depending on my knowledge of running a bakery, there could be a significant learning curve, which represents a learning risk. Not all career decisions are as drastic as this, but when leaders look back and share their wisdom, remarkable growth often follows a significant career risk.

You may never have to make decisions involving a significant level of risk. But, if you do, I hope you'll find some comfort in knowing that many successful leaders approaching the ends of their careers believe that—given the chance again—they'd still take the opportunity with the most perceived risk.

If you find yourself in a similar situation, embrace it!

HOW MANY OF YOUR CAREER BARRIERS ARE FEAR-BASED?

We all experience self-doubt. We all have moments where we question where we're going and if we have what it takes to achieve our dreams. We all list out the reasons things won't work out. We create roadblocks for ourselves. We don't have enough money. We're afraid of letting down people who depend on us. We don't have enough time. We're too old. The list goes on and on. When we list out what's holding us back from chasing our dreams, how many of the reasons are fear-based? I don't know your list, but if it's anything like mine, at least half of the reasons are because I'm afraid of something. I've come to realize this is perfectly normal and almost universal.

Life has a way of teaching us lessons. We see a car speeding through a red light, so we naturally tell ourselves and others to look both ways before crossing the street. We see stories of millionaires who lost all their money due to poor financial management or risky investments, so we are more conservative with our investments and less apt to lend our money to others without a good understanding of how we will be repaid. And most of the time, especially when it comes to money and safety, these are good lessons to learn. However, when it comes to our careers, life's lessons can sometimes prevent us from pursuing our passions out of the fear of the unknown. Let's focus on how fear holds us back.

It's practical to avoid chasing your dreams because you have people to support or other needs to meet. That means you have priorities you've established in life. However, not chasing your dreams because you've predicted the end before you begin or are afraid of failure is simply an opportunity missed. Remember, you either win or learn. You will never fail; you'll only grow.

Take an honest inventory of your dreams and the roadblocks in your way. Decide if you want to take a detour or push right on through.

THERE IS NO PERFECT COMPANY

I've read many articles indicating that the Great Resignation has turned into the Great Regret. In the early days of the COVID pandemic, there were heavy layoffs and furloughs, which gave people a moment in time known as the Great Pause. People spent a lot of time assessing where they were in their lives and where they wanted to go. Then, when the world economy rebounded from the mass layoffs, the Great Resignation followed. Many people left their jobs in search of new opportunities or entirely new paths. Some surveys indicate that, post-COVID, more than 50 percent of people regret leaving their previous company. Let's take the pandemic out of it for a moment. In general, people can regret specific jumps they've made in their careers. We make a leap to find greener pastures only to realize, once there, that we miss what we had.

It's only natural. In many of these situations, people leave companies they've been with for some time. That means they've built up a reputation. They are known in the company. Their work speaks for itself. They know the culture. At some point, all of that is no longer enough. So, when there's a decision to leave—be it for more money, a shorter commute, being closer to family, or a promotion—it seems like the right step.

But starting over can be difficult. You have to rebuild your brand. You must deliver at your job again until people know you do good work. You have to build new relationships. All these things take time. In the process, you may realize the company culture doesn't match your values, or that your new boss is a micromanager. Whether you participated in the Great Resignation and are now experiencing the Great Regret or are still at the same company you've been at for years, the point is to have the proper perspective.

Change is inevitable. No company is perfect, but there can be a company that is perfect for you *at this point in your career journey*. That qualifier at the end is what's important. Maybe it's time for you to supervise others. Maybe it's time for you to travel to a new city. Maybe it is time to make more money. Or maybe it's time to stay put.

It's important to assess and understand where you are in your career journey. Wherever you find yourself, take some time to reflect on what's important to you, what you're willing to live with, and what you're not willing to live with. Think about the non-negotiables and how much risk you're willing to take.

Now go!

Or—depending on your priorities—stay!! ☺

TAKE ADVANTAGE OF OPPORTUNITIES

You only live once! Life is short. Party like it's 1999. YOLO! (I guess I already said that one!) You get the point. As far as I can tell, we only get one go at this thing called life. Our careers are the same, except with your career, you have the opportunity to start over time and again. That gives you a decided advantage when it comes to taking chances.

When I was in college, people weren't taking gap years or spending a year traveling the world. Well, I guess it's possible they were, but none of my friends were. But if I could do it all again, I would travel before settling into a career. But for those of us already in the workforce, it's not too late to create a new adventure!

How many of you have had an opportunity presented to you that you ended up turning down because you would have had to move, end a relationship, or your pay would not have increased? Think through those moments. They were chances that might have led to something extraordinary. I'm not telling you to end your relationship or take less money. But there is power in saying "Yes."

Have you ever had that friend who is always doing something? It seems like they're up to something every night of the week. Then, on a random Wednesday, they call you to see if you want to hang out with them to do whatever they have planned. How often have you turned that person down? Maybe you were worried about getting enough sleep or getting up for work the next day. Maybe you were in the middle of cooking dinner. Whatever the reason, you said no. Or have you said yes? What was the outcome? More often than not, it turns out to be a wonderful time. A time you likely won't forget. A time you almost missed because <insert excuse here>.

Let's apply this to work. What would happen if the next opportunity that came your way, instead of saying "No," you decided to say "Yes!" What if you said yes to the next two or three opportunities that came your way at work? Hard to imagine, right? I don't have a firm answer for you, but I hypothesize you won't regret it.

Careers are funny. They're windy roads. A pivotal moment in my career almost didn't happen because I had at least five good reasons why I shouldn't have said yes. At least, I thought they were good reasons. Looking back, they were just things that allowed me to remain comfortable in my career bubble. I'll never forget when a former boss told me they thought I should apply for a role when I felt I had no business doing so. They presented an opportunity. I applied for it, interviewed, and ultimately did not get the job. What I did get was the confidence to apply to the next big role. Confidence I didn't have before those interviews.

One final consideration on this topic. You could be reading this and thinking, "Opportunities haven't been coming my way. What do I do with that?" I have two thoughts on that matter. The first is to be sure you're open to opportunities. Sometimes we don't see them because we're not paying attention or putting ourselves in a situation to receive them. The second is that if opportunity doesn't come knocking, kick down the door and make your own!

IF YOU DON'T LIKE THE ENDING, WRITE YOUR OWN

Sylvester Stallone has been an action hero in more movies than I can count. His film career spans several decades, and he seems to reinvent himself each decade. I have no idea how much money he has, but I believe the last time I looked, I read somewhere that he was worth hundreds of millions. I have no idea if that is true, but I do know that he wrote his own ending. In the early 1980s, he wrote a movie called *Rocky*. The main character in that movie is, you guessed it, Rocky. Well, before the film became a box-office success and spawned many sequels, Sylvester Stallone was a struggling actor. He took a chance and bet on himself. He made the studio cast him as the main character in the movie. That was a bold move for someone who had very little in the name of brand recognition, but that was how much he believed in himself. Now his name is everywhere. You can probably rifle through your mind and think of a dozen movies he's starred in, and it's all because he wrote his own ending. You might think that's only possible in Hollywood, but I want you to know possible in any career.

Before I was born, my dad was quite successful in business. He had a good-paying job, he was well-liked, and his future seemed to be set. Yet, he wasn't happy with the ending. He could see how the story would end if he stayed on his existing course. It's not how he wanted things to go, and so he decided to change it. He quit his high-paying job and opened a fish shop that would give him a source of income while he attended law school. He finished law school and opened a law practice. Over time, he became one of the most respected attorneys in the state of Kansas. He was one of the few black, successful attorneys in Kansas at the time. The stories he shared with us of the challenges he had to face would be enough to turn most of us away. I can honestly tell you that I'm not sure I would have had the same grit he showed. The thing was, he *knew* he would be successful eventually. Sure, he had many ups and downs—he still does, even to this day. But for several decades, he's practiced law on his terms and without fear.

I admire and respect that my father rewrote his story. He changed his ending. He isn't the only one who can do it. You can do it too! If you look forward and don't like the future you see, change it. Today! Sure, you will need help and support. Inevitably, there will be highs and lows. But just keep in mind that whether you go out on your own, go to a new company, start a new position, or stay in your current role—you are in the driver's seat. If your career is a car, you are its driver. You get to choose the destination. And if you don't like where you're going, you get to change course.

Now, where are you going?

WHAT IF MOST PEOPLE
WANT YOU TO WIN?

In one of my previous companies, we had a forecast process that culminated in a meeting held at the beginning of each month. The preparation for each meeting took weeks. Everyone involved knew that you needed to be prepared for everything going into a session. If you had a great month, you needed to understand why it occurred and what was required for it to happen again. You needed to answer for a bad month and explain what you would do differently to ensure it didn't happen again. The meeting was pure stress, so we spent hours prepping for it. Inevitably, however, as part of the meeting, the financial controller always had a curveball question that hadn't been thought through ahead of time.

As we prepared, we'd try to anticipate the controller's questions. Sometimes we got them right—those were good days! Sometimes we didn't get them right and were left scrambling. After the meeting, we would gather to compile the answers to the questions we hadn't been able to answer. For the first five minutes after the meeting, we'd complain about the controller and wonder why the goal seemed to be to stump us with difficult questions. After we all decompressed with a little grumbling, we'd figure out the answers and then try to anticipate the questions we'd face the following month.

For months, it bothered me that we spent so much time trying to proactively guess how to address the controller's questions. We spent so much time and energy anticipating! Then, I realized the controller was simply doing their job. Once that dawned on me, my entire perspective changed. It went from a meeting I dreaded to one I looked forward to.

We've all had scenarios like this that have played out over our careers. We get asked a difficult question, or a challenging assignment gets put into our lap. Whenever this happens, begin by checking your mindset. Are you assuming positive intent, sabotage, or something in between? While the latter two are certainly possible, I find it to be an incredibly wasteful exercise to determine. What I *have* found useful is assuming that people are coming from a good place. It helps my attitude and overall approach. In talking with others, this perspective helps them as well. If you assume positive intent, you begin to see solutions where there were problems. You ask better questions in determining scope. You're more quickly and easily productive. In other words, you provide yourself with a chance to move past potential barriers toward resolving the issue—whatever it may be.

Someone I used to play basketball with had a great tactic during games. When people booed, yelled, cackled, and otherwise tried to negatively impact him during games, he pretended the sounds were people cheering him on. It allowed him to walk into any arena and see it as a home crowd. Instead of ignoring the crowd, he embraced them. In return, he performed exceptionally well on the road during hostile situation where others would fold. Sometimes, people's intentions toward you won't be great. People are trained to see another's career ambitions as something that might hold them back. But why give any of that energy? Refocus, and you can still find a way to come out on top!

Where do you need to halt the complaints and make a paradigm shift in your response to challenges? Who wants you to win right now?

WORK HARD. BE HUMBLE. TAKE CREDIT.

There is an ever-so-subtle line between bragging about your past successes and humbly sharing your wins with others. When a person crosses the line, you may find that you no longer enjoy being around or listening to that person. However, when people don't cross the line, you likely find them very enjoyable to work with. Whether or not a person has crossed the line is dependent on the eye of the beholder—it's different for everyone. It's interpretive and all comes down to perspective. So, what is a humble person to do?

Let's begin by stating the obvious. We can all agree that working hard is good. Even if someone is seen as a braggart, when they are a hard worker, we tend to acknowledge the work that they put in. This makes me think of two very different former football players in the National Football League (NFL). One player, LaDainian Tomlinson (or LT), was a running back. He simply handed the ball to the referee whenever he scored a touchdown. No celebration. Nothing that said, "Look at me." Just hard work, followed by humility.

On the other hand, there is Terrell Owens (or TO)—an equally gifted wide receiver. His on- and off-the-field antics screamed, "Look at me," but he was a hard worker. Most observers preferred LT's method of scoring and demeanor over TO's, but most would agree both were hard workers. From that perspective, being a hard worker is desirable.

Next is humility. Some of my favorite leaders—in business and on the world stage—are what's known as "servant leaders." They *can take command,* but they usually take the approach of empowering their teams. They *could take the credit* for their great ideas, but they'd rather give praise and recognition to their team for their contributions. These leaders create an environment where you want to do more and give that extra effort. It's their humility that makes them great leaders. The same goes for humble employees.

Humble workers put their heads down and do their job. When they give extra effort and are given praise, they reply with, "It's my job." They don't need the glory because they take pride in their work. In one respect, when you are a supervisor, these are probably the best employees to have on your team. Conversely, when it comes to adequately recognizing them, your job is all that much more difficult. *Because* they don't seek out recognition, *you need to ensure* they receive it. Ask them to think back over the past six to twelve months and summarize their contributions to you. And then you do the same!

I started this chapter by saying it's a thin line between bragging and humility. That said, if you begin with humility, it's doubtful you'll cross the line. What were your accomplishments this year, and who do you need to recognize?

IF YOU HAVE TO ASK, "WHY AM I HERE?"

You already know the answer.

Have you heard the story of the employee who woke up one day and realized they weren't happy in their job or the direction of their career, so they immediately quit? We all have. While I don't encourage anyone to simply walk away from their responsibilities at work with little to no warning, I *do* encourage you to ask yourself where you are going in your career. I also find it a good practice to ask yourself, "Why did I come to work today?" If you take thirty seconds to ponder why you're doing the type of work that you're doing, as well as why you're in your current job, you should walk away with a clear understanding. You'll know if you should remain in that job, on that path, or not. It's that simple.

Try it.

What if you conclude that you like your job and the people you work with, but it's not the direction you want your career to go? What should you do?

What if you hate your job primarily because of your direct supervisor but like the company culture? What action should you take?

What if you like your job and the direction it's taking you in your career, and the company culture is great, but in talking with peers, you realize there's a good chance you're underpaid? What's your next step?

Each of these situations highlights what should be an obvious next step. When we take the time to pause from the daily grind of our careers, and put ourselves first, we know what we need to do next. Instead of tending to ourselves regularly, what tends to happen is that we suffer or stress over time. Then, we become frustrated and resentful until we finally find ourselves asking, "Why am I here?" But there is another way.

You can stop well before the boiling point and make time to take inventory of yourself. Ask yourself, "Where am I going? Why did I come to work? Why am I at this company? What career value am I gaining in my job?" If you ask these questions regularly, you'll find that you can better maneuver through your career journey before you reach the tipping point.

How would you answer these questions today?

NOT ALL STARS WANT TO MANAGE

Don't make them.

This is a straightforward topic—yet I think it's worth mentioning. Suppose you are given the privilege to lead others. In that case, you owe it to yourself and your team to take inventory of your willingness and capability to manage their career needs. By that I mean, you must be honest about whether you can put your team's recognition, outcomes, and development needs in front of your own. This is sometimes easier said than done. People often believe that when they've hit a certain level of success in an organization that they should become a manager.

A classic example of this you will often see in organizations is the star salesperson. This individual could sell anything to anyone and is excellent at their job. In many companies, to move ahead, they will require that the salesperson become a manager—effectively moving from an individual contributor to a supervisor. And it's here they fail miserably. The thing that motivated them—the hunt for new business is taken away.

What's more, they have to put their energy into developing a team so that *the team* can become great at sales. When a newly promoted manager has no enthusiasm or desire to be a coach, it's likely they won't be good at it. To make matters worse, *because* they aren't good at coaching others, their past accomplishments are overlooked; then there's a question if this person is suitable for the organization.

Okay, let's take a time out. There's a lot to unpack in this scenario. First, hopefully, organizations are evolving enough to realize that not all career paths are created the same. There are some outstanding individual contributors. If the only option for them to get promoted is being a manager, be honest with them about what it takes to be a successful manager.

Second, if there are alternatives that allow them to move forward without managing, *tell them*. If there aren't such options, think about whether or not there should be. Be the first to suggest it and try it out.

I chose salespeople as the example here because it's one that I see most often, but this is relevant across all functions and positions. If you find yourself in a place where you are a superstar individual contributor without the desire to manage others, have an honest conversation with yourself and your supervisor. I *have* seen reluctant, successful individual contributors became fantastic managers, so don't rush to resist the potential. At the same time, if you do decide to move forward, gauge your enthusiasm and effectiveness *early and often*.

Whether this is about you or someone you lead: Keep an open mind, and try something new, but be honest about what motivates you. Pursue your passion, as that is ultimately where you are most likely to win. Good luck!

SMILE. YOU'D BE SURPRISED WHAT HAPPENS NEXT.

You wake up, and the alarm is blaring. It's the fourth time you hit snooze. You have a key meeting that you've been dreading all week. After you shower, you still feel tired. As you think about the moments leading up to the meeting, you start having gnawing feelings of anxiety. What are you to do?

Smile!

I'm not a doctor, and I haven't been trained in either physiology or neurology. But I can tell you that something happens when we smile. The physical action of smiling does something in our brains. Try it. If you live near a city or by a busy sidewalk, try walking down the street without saying anything and simply smile at everyone you pass. What's the first thing you realize? Likely that quite a few people smile back at you. What's the other thing that happens? You'll probably feel a positive vibe back from the smile they give you! It's like magic. And here's the thing—this same approach works at work too!

I've been the person in the first paragraph. I can distinctly recall having days like that. Days during the work week that caused me stress. Meetings that used to give me anxiety. Over time, several things happened. First, I found work that I was passionate about. Naturally, I wanted to excel in an area I enjoyed. Second, I realized that only so much could come out of any meeting. Sure, I could fall flat on my face at any meeting—that's true. But even if that does happen, there are lessons for me to learn. If I prepared, but just not enough, I'll prepare better next time. If my supervisor gives me coaching and feedback on how to improve, I'll take the feedback and get better. The point is that if I'm doing something I enjoy and need to improve, I want to do it. Lastly, if I overthink the situation, there's a good chance that I will think the bad stuff into reality.

Ever coach someone at a sport and catch yourself saying things like "don't do that" during the game? What inevitably happens? They do whatever it was you told them *not to do*. But if you spin it and ask them, "What are you thinking about the exact moment when *this* happens," they reflect on the variables in the situation and eventually work their way through what's holding them back. At least most of the time! The point is that negative thoughts can lead to negative outcomes.

It's hard to be negative when you're smiling. Think about what you enjoy about your job, a funny anecdote, or even something non-work related to break up the angst and self-doubt. Let whatever it is ease your tension, and then let go of it altogether. Do your best and be comfortable that you will continue to improve *whatever the outcome.*

What do you need to smile about today?

IT'S OKAY TO ASK FOR HELP

Who in their entire career has accomplished their goals entirely by themselves? That's a person I want to meet so that I can understand their methods. My guess is if you walked into any company in the world and asked that question to a roomful of people, no one would raise their hand. It's nearly impossible to achieve your career goals without someone's help. So, why is it so hard to ask for help sometimes?

When we attend conferences or seminars, a lot of times, we're looking to learn. We're looking to benchmark other companies or better understand the secrets leaders in other organizations utilize to create wins. We're willing to pay for those lessons, and often for good reason. If we come away from these events with two or three good ideas that can be put into practice, it's usually considered a worthwhile investment. Then why is it difficult to ask others for assistance or guidance when we are back in our everyday work environment?

Sometimes we hesitate to reach out because we don't really know the person that could likely assist us. Maybe they're in a different business within your organization, or perhaps you've never been introduced. It could seem like a barrier if you're not naturally inclined to introduce yourself. Other times, we're not even aware that we need help! So, why would we ask for help if we don't know it's required? Other times we do know we need help, and we know a person who could help, but we believe we can do it on our own—so why bother someone else? I've spoken with numerous professionals who have experienced all the scenarios I've just listed. In the end, do you know what they all needed? *Help from others.*

I encourage you to regularly bounce your career ideas off of people you know. Ask them to connect you to people they know for even more advice and insight. You'd be surprised to learn that the more extensive your career network, the more solutions tend to appear with greater ease. You're talking to a peer about one situation, and they share something similar they've seen or experienced. You mention your challenge, and they give you another name to follow up with. And you should follow up! Getting assistance is an opportunity to create shared experiences while growing professionally.

Take advantage of it!

I GUARANTEE YOU: SOMEONE DESERVES IT LESS

Have you ever had someone walk over to you looking sheepish, so you decide to ask, "What's wrong?" With furrowed eyebrows and a half-smile on their face, they tell you, "I got a promotion." It's almost as if they feel bad about it! As a coach, I've had some form of this conversation so many times. People often feel undeserving of the promotion, the praise, or recognition for a job well done. Usually, these individuals come from a good place. They're humble and work hard but have difficulty accepting the praise or raise they are given. These are some of my favorite career discussions because we're typically talking about someone very deserving.

If you recognize this type of exchange—maybe you rarely feel deserving, or perhaps you know someone who doesn't feel deserving—then I want you to close your eyes and try to imagine a scenario for me. No, wait, never mind. This is a book. Open your eyes again so you can read the rest of this chapter! Imagine I am Robin Williams, and you are Matt Damon in *Good Will*

Hunting. Instead of saying, "It's not your fault," listen to me as I tell you, "You deserve this."

"I know."

"You deserve this."

"I know!"

"You deserve this."

"I KNOW!"

You deserve the goodwill that comes your way. Pun intended. Learn to embrace it and use it to continue the positive momentum. From time to time, all of us are prone to thinking that we didn't earn whatever good comes our way. However, success is an outcome of many different variables, and effort is a primary driver.

Make the most of it! Help others. Heap praise on those who supported you. Lift others around you. Because I can guarantee you there are others that deserve it less, so soak it up!

And watch *Good Will Hunting*. Let me know if that particular scene isn't one of the best movie scenes . . . like, ever!

YOUR TIME IS VALUABLE TOO!

It doesn't matter where you sit in an organization or company: Your time has worth. I typically don't read a lot of tabloids, but I do watch movies. Every once in a while, it seems that movies, actors, and tabloids seem to collide. One of those times was with the "Fast and the Furious" series. Allegedly, there was a beef between Dwayne "The Rock" Johnson and Vin Diesel. I never fully heard Vin Diesel's side of it, but Dwayne Johnson boiled it down to being a professional. It seemed like Vin Diesel would come onto the set late, and everyone would be waiting for him. Now, I don't know what's true or not, so I'll leave it to the tabloids to determine the truth. But it does demonstrate the point of valuing others' time.

Have you ever worked with a boss who was habitually late, so meetings didn't start unless they arrived? What about just a senior leader with the same penchant? Early in my career, my boss and I would visit one of our clients and we'd have meetings in their office. The entire time we presented our findings, the client would be reading e-mails on their computer or looking at their phone. We'd ask a question, and the answers were monosyllabic because they'd be focused on a screen reading something. It was a mess! Inevitably we had to repeat things many times over. The client was a nice enough person, but they had no concept of how they were coming across. Over time, our client base changed, and I no longer had to support that person, but I took a valuable lesson from those meetings. Since then, if I'm hosting a meeting or if someone is in my office, I stop what I'm doing and give them my full attention. If I cannot do that, I either share the current priority or seek to reschedule. It's a simple approach. The best leaders understand that everyone's time is valuable!

This applies across organizational hierarchies and levels. I know a leader who used to have to hire a lot of people. This person would have their administrative assistant schedule the interviews and greet the candidates. The jobs were essential and often carried some challenging requirements, which could be stressful at times. After the interview, the supervisor would ask the administrative assistant for their take on every interviewee. They were looking to understand how the candidate performed before, during, and after the interview. In essence, the administrative assistant was part of the interview. I've known leaders who do something similar with the cleaning staff and other workers at all levels of the organization. These leaders value the time and input of *all of their employees,* and their organizational cultures reflect those values.

This week, pay attention to how your time is treated. Is it with respect and value or not? Does anything need to change?

PEOPLE *ARE* LOOKING TO YOU FOR ANSWERS

The senior leader walks into the room, lays out a complicated situation, and asks the team for possible solutions. You're not entirely familiar with the problem, but you immediately get a few ideas; however, you decide to remain quiet. There's an awkward silence in the room. The leader proceeds to map out a path toward a resolution. The moment is gone. Immediately after your meeting, one of your direct reports asks you why you didn't share the idea you had mentioned to them a couple of weeks earlier. In development conversations a few months later, the leadership team is gathered in the room to discuss up-and-coming leaders in the organization. One of them mentions your name briefly, but no one else speaks up, with the consensus being that none of them really know you—nor have they seen you step up on the more meaningful projects. Others around you see your potential as a leader, so why don't you?

I'll let you in on a secret—many top leaders in organizations don't have all the answers. In fact, many of the ones I know *don't want to know* all the answers. Their goal is to build a strong team around them who can provide them with answers. Many people prefer to gather a team of diverse minds that are capable of leading organizations. In other words, leaders could be looking to you for answers, and you should ask yourself if you're prepared to give them what they are looking for!

There was a time when the company's president or senior-most leader was expected to have all the answers. Everyone knew they were the most intelligent person in the room when they walked in. While there are still companies run that way, many top organizations today realize that two or three minds are better than one. Leaders today surround themselves with fantastic talent and know that they may only have them for a short while, so they better challenge them and utilize their insights while they have them. Be that talented leader people want on their teams!

You don't have to speak up on every occasion, but if you have an answer, you should speak up. Some of the most brilliant, creative people I know hesitate to share their opinions. Great leaders will find a way to capture the insights of such individuals, but then you're at the leader's mercy. Own it!

How are you creating value? If you're good at something in the company, find a way to share it with your boss and other leaders. Start practicing today!

INSPIRATIONS

ADMIRE PROBLEMS.
CREATE SOLUTIONS.

Have you ever been on a team where one person is the absolute best about telling you everything wrong with the current situation? They list all the internal and external forces lined up to make it an unwinnable environment. And, to top it off, they're right! The only issue with highlighting all these problems is that they do not have a solution. However right they may be, if they're only able to identify a problem without providing a solution, there's a good chance it can negatively impact their career. Conversely, if you are known in your organization as a problem-solver, you may be opening future career doors.

Don't get me wrong—there is a benefit to having someone on your team who can correctly and quickly identify issues within the organization. These individuals can save countless hours and frustration by simply summarizing a known issue. It's even better if that person can take it one step further and has already begun proposing solutions. Across my career, I've seen real "fixers" all over. The chemist in research and development who solves a challenging customer-quality issue. The sales representative who seals the deal on an agreement that will make up the revenue shortfall from the beginning of the year. The customer service representative who stays on the phone with the client until the issue is resolved. These people are worth their weight in gold to organizations because they help companies win. And the beauty of it all is that anyone might be a solution finder.

I haven't cornered the market on recognizing the traits of team members who are great at creating solutions. But I've noticed a few key traits that "fixers" have:

- **They're passionate about their job:** Often, they spend a significant amount of brainpower on whatever issue is ailing the company. I've also seen one or two employees who enlist the help of countless others until the answer to a problem has revealed itself. They enjoy their work so much that it's not problem-solving; it is simply enjoying the work they do every day.

- **They are knowledgeable:** They are the resident expert. They are known in the company, the industry, and possibly the world as the person to see when you need a solution.

- **They are creative:** This is the clincher about these individuals. They see possibilities in things most people find ordinary. Because they see the world through the lens of options, they can piece together ideas in ways not previously explored.

Who is this person in your organization?
What would it take for this person to be you?

IT'S OKAY TO BE AFRAID OF SUCCESS, BUT DON'T LET IT STOP YOU!

What if your wildest career dreams came true? What would you do? You're about to interview for your dream job, and it's down to you and another candidate. You tend to speak fast when you're nervous. They call you into the interview, and your heart is pounding. Using a sports analogy, you're down by one, and you're at the free-throw line. You made your first shot, and the next one could win the game. So many professionals and players miss the shot. Why? They're thinking of all the ways the situation could go wrong instead of everything they've done that's led them to this moment. They freeze, and it causes them to miss.

There's a whole psychology to it that I'm not qualified to provide detail on. But I can tell you that when this happens, people have gotten stuck in their own heads. They're so busy focusing on the negative that they forget their form or talk too fast—whatever tactic they automatically use to navigate the fear of success with which they are faced. Instead of trying to deny or compartmentalize the fear, embrace it. Invite it in.

I coach basketball. One of the most challenging situations is when the other team decides to put a full-court press on your team. That means they guard you from the moment you inbound the ball, and they continue applying pressure until it causes you to lose the ball. When you eventually turn the ball over, they're able to score easy buckets. Want to know one of the best ways to beat the press? *Attack* the pressure. The individuals pressing you know what they *want you to do*, but until you make a move, they have no idea what you *will* do. If you attack the press faster than it can get set up, you can catch them off guard and score an easy bucket for your team. Another way to beat a press is to invite the pressure. When you force the other team's defense to show their hand, it gives you time to decide how to beat it. The *worst way* to beat a press is to run away from it or panic. You will almost certainly lose the ball to the other team. Experience like this comes with time; it requires being in pressure-filled situations repeatedly.

Career presses are similar. Moments in our careers that are filled with pressure can lead to opportunities. Moments to shine, grow, learn, prosper, and grow accustomed to pressure—but only if you *work with them* instead of against them. Success comes from putting yourself in a situation again and again until you're comfortable with the pressure. Afraid of interviews? Ask an HR friend to drill you on interviews until you start to get good at it. Look for ways to practice and get used to scenarios until you master them.

It's okay to be afraid of success, but don't let that stop you!

INSPIRE

There is greatness inside of all of us. I believe this with all my being. Each of us has a gift that's been bestowed exclusively to us. It's common for other people to see our gift before we recognize it. But sometimes, we're lucky enough to know what it is early and start to develop it. At work, there is always a supervisor who is great at developing others. There's the salesperson who can sell anything. There is the president who captures the hearts and minds of the entire team every time they speak. The visionary entrepreneur who sees a future so clearly that others see it too. There's the HR professional who gives you just the right advice at just the right time. The finance professional who can pull together insightful spreadsheets on your business that save you time and money. The senior leader who seems to know what you're going to say before you say it. There's the author whose books inspire people to live their best lives. The list goes on and on.

Find your gift and share it. I imagine a world where all of us do just that—make the lives of others better. I'm a sucker for the stories where a famous person does something nice for someone when they are young, and that young person goes on to do amazing things and shares the moment with others. When people recognize how others have influenced them and pay it forward, that's truly special. It helps people make the most of what's uniquely *them* and do the same for others. At work and in life, there is way more positive than negative, even if it doesn't make the news.

Shine your light! Lift up others around you. Inspire!

YOU WERE HELPED.
THANK THEM.

This one is obvious. We all stood on someone's shoulders to get where we are today. Maybe you don't like where you are today; but imagine not having the two or three people who brought you to this point. How much worse could it have been? Most of us have had someone, or several someones, guide us in ways that have had a profound impact on our lives. I had a third-grade teacher tell me that I was a good speller. Do you know that, to this day, I take pride in my ability to spell? Maybe a friend introduced you to someone who helped you get your dream job. Perhaps the boss stuck their neck out and you were promoted into a position you may not have been fully qualified for at the time. Maybe a parent or guardian supported you through college to the best of their ability and provided you with an education that would last throughout your career. We all have people who have helped us. And they all deserve our thanks.

It's easy to think that if we find success, the success is of our own creation. In many ways, we are encouraged to believe we were able to overcome all of life's challenges by ourselves. People love a good "bootstrapped" story, but these perspectives are usually shortsighted and incorrect. Acknowledging those who have helped you along the way is very grounding. The truth is that so many people join you on your career journey. Some are there for the beginning of the trip. A few will join you for one or two stops only. A select few will be there for most of the ride. But make no mistake, you're never on the voyage alone. So, thank them.

The people who helped you along the way are invested in you. Tell them of your current struggles. Share your successes with them. Highlight them in the good times. Remember them during difficult times. Your story helps their story. You'd be surprised at how meaningful two words are to those around you. So don't hoard gratitude or success. Share it. Share it like it was shared with you.

YOU WERE HELPED. HELP SOMEONE.

In the comic books, Spiderman's uncle tells him something like, "Upon whom much is given, much is required." In other words, if you've been given a lot, you need to give a lot back. In the comics, it helps Spiderman find his focus. In your career, it allows you to share your knowledge with others.

Hit the pause button on the race of life and reflect people who took time to assist you in some aspect of your career. I can imagine the list is long. Now think of a younger version of you out there somewhere who needs that same support. Every day, a younger you joins the workforce. They join your company. They join your team. They may not even know they need your guidance, but they do. Now look around and see who that person is. Who are they? How will you get involved? How will you help?

What are your strengths? Are they well-known to others? Do people reach out to learn from you? Have you spoken to others about ways you can assist them? Have you volunteered your time, expertise, insights, or support? Some people say, "I'm not a coach like you." My response is, "Of course, you're not a coach like me. Being a coach *like me* is impossible as I'm the only me. But you can be a coach *like you!*" A lot of people think because they haven't been told they're good at this or that, it means they don't have something to give. I disagree. We all have something to offer. Even if that *something* is just all the mistakes we've made along the way! Sharing knowledge of past failures may be more important than sharing successes. Don't think for one minute that you don't have something to give. You do!

Who needs your career perspective today?

GO AHEAD, END ALL YOUR MEETINGS FIVE MINUTES EARLY THIS WEEK!

I've read so many books and articles about maximizing how we use our time that I'm sure I can recite some of the best ones from memory. So, why is it that more and more of these books are bestsellers each year? Because clearly, no one is fully listening to them! I say this tongue-in-cheek, but I would guess there is a bit of truth in the statement. Have you ever been in a meeting that could have ended twenty minutes earlier, but for some reason, it carried on for a full hour? We've all had this happen at least once. Generally, I think that if a meeting is scheduled for an hour, many people think it can't end even one minute early. You'd think the meeting organizer was the primary time culprit. However, it's difficult to pin responsibility to only one person. There's the person who asks really good questions that aren't relevant to the meeting. Or the person who wants to explore potential solutions by brainstorming in a meeting that was simply an information-sharing session. There are so many reasons for meetings carrying on longer than they need to or not being a good use of time. On behalf of all those time-management books I've devoured, I ask you to give five minutes back this week. Just five minutes. For one week, end all your meetings five minutes early.

It seems so innocuous on the surface. Only five minutes? That's not that long. How hard can it be? You'd be surprised. After the first meeting on Monday, you'll think this will be a cakewalk. In your mind, you're thinking of all the meetings you are hosting, and it crosses your mind that you can control the outcome of each of these meetings. You'll have no problem accomplishing the feat in a week. Then it dawns on you who you've invited to the meetings. Now you realize there is a nearly zero percent chance that you will be able to complete the task *even if you host the meetings.* What's even more difficult is when you realize I am referring to ALL meetings that happen in a week—whether you are the host or not. How do you control the time of meetings when you are not the clear driver of the meeting? And this is where the fun begins.

I've only challenged you to one task—end your meetings five minutes early. I did not give you the parameters by which you measure success. There are several different ways to interpret the challenge to find success. If you only have one meeting this week, I'm asking you to find five minutes. If you have twenty meetings this week, I'm asking you to find one hour. How will you do it? Do me a favor. When you have a moment, send me an e-mail to Ha-Keem@CoachHa-Keem.com and let me know how it goes. If I get enough varied responses, I may publish them in an article or possibly even another book. We'll call it *You're Worth It! I'm Only Asking for Five Minutes of Your Time.* Or something clever like that.

The clock starts now!

IF YOU KNEW A CAREER MOVE WOULD BE 100 PERCENT SUCCESSFUL

Would you do it?

What about 75 percent? What about 60 percent? What. Are. You. Waiting. For?

I worked for a small business line that was part of a larger organization. The smaller company was moving at the speed of an entrepreneurial business, but it was part of a larger entity with rules, guidelines, and procedures. These rules were established to minimize the entire company's risk exposure. The smaller business was a calculated risk, so the larger company had increased scrutiny to offset that risk. It came to a point where to offset the smaller company's business risk, the larger organization nearly destroyed the smaller company's growth. Now, the good news was that both organizations were performing well, but there are career lessons we can all learn from what they went through. If we are waiting for 100 percent certainty before making a move that might advance ourselves or help us grow, we may be metaphorically killing our careers. We'll be waiting a long time if that's our risk threshold.

Yet, that's the very sentiment expressed by several successful people with whom I've had the pleasure of working:

- "I'm not ready to apply for that position."

- "Once I see this three-year project to completion, I'll be ready for a move."

- "I don't meet all of the criteria for that role even though I know someone with the same background is applying."

We're waiting for the perfect time to act when there is no perfect time. The time to act is now! I can think of quite a long list of things I'd try if I knew I would be 100 percent successful. It would be a shorter list if I knew the odds were fifty-fifty. Why is the list shorter? In truth, it's because I don't want to waste my time, cause financial ruin (I have big dreams), or fail. My desire to avoid failure probably informs a lot of my decisions.

My first book was a lifetime in the making. I had always wanted to write a book. I dabbled in writing throughout high school and some in college. Then I grew up. I was an adult, and life got in the way. I needed to be responsible. I didn't have time to write. If I spent time writing a book that didn't perform well, it would be a waste. All of those things kept me from writing a book. The other day someone came up to me and told me she'd been promoted three times since reading my book *You're Worth It! Navigating Your Career in Corporate America*. Her feedback gave me chills because I almost didn't write the book. I'm so glad I did. If it helped one person, that's enough for me.

You will be great! You will not fail because your mindset is winning or learning. Failure is not in the cards for you today, which means you'll be 100 percent successful.

Now, what are you going to do?

YOU ARE AWESOME. NOW PROVE IT!

We all have a backstory or origin story. If you don't know what I'm referring to, think back to the part of any hero-driven movie. There's always a part of the movie where the hero's history is reviewed. The film typically shows all the tribulations the hero endured before reaching a pivotal stretch in their life or journey. Well, you are the main character in your movie. You are the hero! Your own trials led you to where you are today. Each of us arrives at our career nexus differently, but the journey there reveals a lot: we're capable of more than we think!

Think about it. You may have had a difficult childhood. Maybe you grew up with little or no money. Maybe you're in a single-parent household. Maybe you finished high school and didn't go on to college. Maybe you are still working to get that high school diploma. Maybe you've had to support your siblings. Maybe you've had to support your parents or currently anticipate that day is coming. No matter your background, you've come a long way already.

What's more, there are still ways for you to grow. And I mean it. If you're reading this and you're ninety-nine, you have an opportunity to make a difference in the lives of so many people who are earlier in their careers.

I want you to grab a piece of paper and write down all the accomplishments that you've had up to this point in your personal life. Now write down all of your career accomplishments—even if you're just starting. List out everything that had to happen to make both sets of accomplishments possible. Starting to see the picture?

Amazingly, even with all of that written down, some of you will look at the list and either think it's not enough or nothing special. I'm here to tell you that *it is* special. You are special! Each of us has a gift, and your gift is unique to you. Maybe you haven't fully wrapped your arms around your gift. If you're unsure of what it is, ask someone close to you—a friend or a family member. You'll be surprised at the answers that come forth. Sometimes we don't see the light inside each of us that can push us forward in our careers, but others do. It's my personal mission to help the people I meet see within themselves all that I see.

You are awesome.

Now prove it!

WHAT DO YOU WISH PEOPLE WOULD SAY ABOUT YOU? DO THAT.

He was passionate. She followed her dreams. She made everyone better. He was the best at what he did. She was the go-to person. On and on, the accolades go. But as you reflect on your current career—how do your colleagues refer to you? For this, I'm referring to more than your brand. I'm referring to your career legacy. When you imagine the highlight reel you've built up by the end of your career, what will it say about you? What do you wish people would say about you? Don't wait another minute—do that!

I remember my first job. I fried fish at Long John Silvers, and I loved it. I wanted to do a great job every time, and I was proud to serve all of the customers. As I was preparing to return to school, my supervisor told me that I was a hard worker and offered me more money. All these years later, I take pride in being a hard worker. Is that how people refer to me? I hope so—but I'm not waiting around to find out. Too busy!

It's also never too late to start over. I'm not talking about mistakes, though I personally believe in second chances after mistakes. Assuming our mistakes didn't harm others, most of us deserve another shot. No one would want to be judged for our worst moments—careerwise or other. When I say start over, I'm referring to making a career change. Sometimes we resist making a change because we believe we've already invested too much time in a field.

Hogwash, I say!

I have a good family friend who started their career in accounting. They were successful. Somewhere along their career, they decided they didn't want to stay in accounting. They wanted to be independent and have flexible hours, so they went into real estate. They were successful there too, but after losing weekends for so many years, they decided they liked working with people. After exploring the legal side of real estate, they joined an organization's accounting department, but then leveraged their company accounting network to land an HR job within the company. Later, they leveraged their HR experiences to become a chief human resources officer! Lesson: It's never too late to start over or follow your dreams.

What dream are you not realizing at this very moment? What has to be true for you to begin? Do it!

BE ORIGINAL. BE POSITIVE!

You're probably thinking to yourself, "I AM original! There is only ONE me!" If so, you're probably thinking you've figured out and dominated this section before we even began. You might be right! If any of you have completed *StrengthsFinder,* now known as *CliftonStrengths* by Gallup, then you're familiar with how they have you take an assessment to uncover your top strengths. One of my top strengths, according to that assessment, is individualization. An oversimplified summary is that I tend not to stereotype people and see their uniqueness. I walk into work, and I am genuinely amazed by how great each person is. I see:

- The single mom working and feeding her entire family while putting herself through school. Beautiful!

- The Dutchman who speaks French, works in an English-speaking country, is married, and has a farm. Wonderful!

- The African-American woman who does not feel seen, heard, or respected by her supervisors simply because of her gorgeous skin tone. I see you!

- The Asian woman who is told she looks like a child because she has incredible genetics and remains youthful. You are an amazing professional regardless of your age or appearance!

- The white male who asks his colleagues with different skin tones how they are doing after a traumatizing race-related event. Splendid!

So many glorious people with absolutely inspiring backgrounds. You be you! Bring your whole self to work. If you can't do that, you should first check that it isn't *you* holding yourself back. Often, someone will say their work or boss wasn't accepting of who they were as a person, only to find out their supervisor never knew that was an issue. If something is important to you, and you don't know how people at work feel or think about it, make sure you give them a chance.

There's something embedded in all of this that I hope we all strive to do every day. Be positive! If you look at the news, you'd think the world is filled with only terrible people. I'm here to tell you that the world is mostly full of good people. Even more, when people are on the verge of having a good or bad day, and you could be the difference in their day. The smile you give them in the hallway. The door you hold open for them. The elevator you ensure doesn't close. The assumption was that the intent of their e-mail was a positive. These things make a difference at work and in personal lives. We are all bringing something from home to work. Be the person who helps work be a safe place and a refuge from all the difficulties in life.

Be yourself! Spread joy!

YOU MAY SEE A FUTURE
NO ONE ELSE DOES

Have you ever woken up and realized that your long-held dreams are totally out of sync with what you are scheduled to do that day? Moments like these can lead to a lot of self-reflection. Memories may pop up of past conversations with well-intended friends and family about what *they thought* the right career for you was. I love reading about significant historical figures. It always amazes me how often they were on a very solitary path because others did not share in their vision for the future.

I've met a brilliant scientist who retired to make cheese. I've spoken with a successful trader who became a farmer. I know a successful childcare professional who is now an owner of a plumbing company. I read about a successful American football player who abruptly stopped his career to help others as a doctor. In all of these situations, I'm sure there were more than a few people who wondered if they were making the right decision. It's possible that even some of those individuals told them they were making the wrong decision for their lives. But that's the thing about owning your career decisions: You're the one who lives with the consequences—for better or worse.

Why is there the term "struggling actor" or "struggling artist?" Maybe it's because there are so many of them, but it's also likely that these individuals are so committed to following their dreams. They are willing to go *all in*. Dwayne "The Rock" Johnson is famous for saying that he had seven dollars in his pocket before he began to catch some breaks in his career. What if someone told him that his dream of becoming a professional wrestler was a waste of time? Today he is one of the most successful former wrestlers of all time. He is a bonafide movie star and now owns his own brand of tequila. Pretty good, too, if I might add!

The point here is pretty simple. Just because others don't understand where you're going or want to go in your career, that doesn't mean you're heading in the wrong direction. It's like everything else: We all must live with our choices. That may mean we sacrifice some things to pursue a path, and we must live with whatever those are. But be true to yourself. Quite a few people have shared with me that as they were nearing retirement their one regret had to be not doing *this* or *that* early in their career.

If this regret is still with them after all of those years, it tells me that it's much better to pursue your career passion and "fail" than not pursue it and "succeed."

BET ON YOURSELF—YOU'RE WORTH IT!

If you've read all the advice, insights, and inspirations to this point, you're likely bursting at the seams with all the ways you will be blazing a bright future! I genuinely hope that is the case. In reality, many of these will take time to enact. Once you string a few of them together, they will get easier to do so you can repeat them again and again. The time you spend on yourself is an investment. We work. We put our money into markets with the hope that our money will accrue interest over time, and eventually, we'll be able to retire with enough money in our accounts to do whatever we want. The safest bet is with you— betting on yourself!

If no one else believes in you, know that I do! Even if you don't believe in you, I do! It doesn't matter where you *think* you are in your career, the reality is that you've only just begun. Success is right around the corner, but define success how *you* want to define it. It doesn't have to be fancy cars or big bank accounts. It can be helping one person find success. It can be the smile that made someone's day or the teacher you thanked.

The wins are all around you. Go get them. You're worth it!

THE NEXT CHAPTER

If you've read all of the sections of this book, you've armed yourself with the key advice, insights, and inspirations that I've learned over the years. My sincere hope is that they assist you on your career journey.

While the advice is relatively simple—keep track of your accomplishments, remember to breathe, be kind to others, etc.— it's in the practice of these suggestions that I believe you will find the most benefit.

The book has more insights than advice—thirty-five kernels of insight versus twenty-four pieces of advice. One reason for that is that I only have so much advice to give! I'm always hesitant to give advice, because I don't want to appear as if I'm preaching what's right and wrong. I simply want to share useful information that has been passed to me or that I learned over time. As I mentioned before, we all have doubts! Insights, however, are nuggets of wisdom that are less directive. While prescriptive advice can seem very "do this" or "don't do that," insights allow us to glean what's useful and apply it to our own lives. Insights are opportunities to reflect on what's important to you, so I'm happy to share and do hope you find them useful.

Finally, the inspirations. I hope these help you see the *you that you can be for others*. I believe we all can be a beacon of light for others. It's the attitude of gratitude. No matter where you are in life—whether it's where you want to be or you're not quite there yet—we can lift up others around us. To be of service to others, we've got to reflect on who needs our light; then, we must shine a light on them as it was done for us. I didn't fully grasp this responsibility until I started this second book and realized I coach differently depending on the situation. Sometimes I'm a career coach, and sometimes I'm a career cheerleader. We all need someone who lifts us up and helps us find the best version of ourselves. With this book, I've tried to pay it forward. I hope I've lifted you in the same way I've been lifted across my life and career. I also hope that you do the same for others.

You're ready.

You always have been ready. Now, I
hope you *know* you're ready!

Take that next step in your career
development. Because you're worth it!

Coach Ha-Keem

ABOUT THE AUTHOR

Ha-Keem Abdel-Khaliq is currently a Vice President in Human Resources. This book is his second book in the **You're Worth It** series. His first book in the series, *You're Worth It! Navigating Your Career in Corporate America,* was the culmination of a life-long dream. Ha-Keem is an accomplished international speaker, having been invited to present at workshops, corporate events, business clubs, and other professional events.

With nearly thirty years of professional experience, he's worked at some of the world's largest global companies. He has been an HR leader for almost two decades, counseled hundreds of employees in their careers, conducted thousands of interviews, and reviewed 100,000+ resumes.

In his free time, he coaches basketball, is a movie addict, loves 80s music, and writes both fiction and non-fiction books. He lives with his wife and two kids in Minneapolis, Minnesota. Ha-Keem cites his active imagination and personal experiences as the inspiration for much of his writing, which he envisions as a source of joy for his beloved wife, Erica.

He believes watching and internalizing many of the concepts from *The Matrix* will better your life. And, if you're around him long enough, you'll realize that at least fifty percent of his movie quotes are from the 90s classics *The Usual Suspects, Good Will Hunting, Training Day, and Pulp Fiction.*

You can connect with Ha-Keem through his website:

www.CoachHa-Keem.com